The Giver

Doug Wing

For permission requests, write to the publisher, addressed "Attention: Permissions Coordinator," carol@markvictorhansenlibrary.com

Quantity sales special discounts are available on quantity purchases by corporations, associations, and others. For details, contact the publisher at carol@markvictorhansenlibrary.com

Orders by U.S. trade bookstores and wholesalers. Email: carol@markvictorhansenlibrary.com

Creative contribution by Mike Vreeland
Cover Design - Low & Joe Creative, Brea, CA 92821
Book Layout - DBree, StoneBear Design

Manufactured and printed in the United States of America distributed globally by markvictorhansenlibrary.com

New York | Los Angeles | London | Sydney

ISBN: 979-8-88581-050-0 Hardback
ISBN: 979-8-88581-051-7 Paperback
ISBN: 979-8-88581-052-4 eBook
Library of Congress Control Number: 2022914863

Contents

Foreword

Most people live an entire lifetime and never have the good fortune of meeting someone like Doug Wing. I have not only had the privilege of meeting him, but I also have the honor of calling him one of my best friends.

This book is based on one of the most powerful principles upon which a person can model their life. Not only does giving impact lives, it can change them completely. The concept of being a giver is not new by any stretch of the imagination. It's as timeless as planet earth itself. What makes this story so unique is the essence and heart of the giver. It is when we give with no expectation or desire for reward that we truly find meaning in the act of giving. It becomes who we are and not just what we do.

Such is the case in *The Giver*, a heartwarming story about a man who gives on a different level than anyone I've ever known. It's an insider's view of the life of a man who sets an example for his children and helps shape his community with acts of kindness, compassion, and generosity and also by offering opportunity. The Giver demonstrates to us all the power of helping others and doing it in a mostly anonymous and selfless way.

This book is a real page turner. Every chapter will leave you touched and inspired. As you read this book, I hope you will find yourself looking for ways to apply

this same energy and attitude to your own life. You may be surprised how you are impacted as a result.

Life can certainly be challenging at times. This amazing book is a great reminder of how we can redirect our energy and circumvent some of the challenges in our own lives by applying the principles of giving to others. It also provides a philosophical road map to help us each leave a legacy that will positively impact generations to come.

Ken Walls, author of #1 bestseller *Walls of Wisdom: Turning Pain Into Profit*

Prologue

I have been blessed with an extraordinary life and I will ever be grateful for the wisdom, experience, and example my father showed me throughout my life.

This book is written as a tribute to him and his life of generosity. He never wanted praise and he expected nothing in return. His life was helping people in unexpected ways and making their lives better.

My wish is that everyone can learn from Spencer's journey and how transformative life can be when we focus on others.

CHAPTER 1

Business

Spencer Ward hung up the phone, stood up from his plush leather office chair, and walked over to the large picture window of his second-floor office. He leaned forward and rested his forehead on the cool glass to soothe his pulsing veins. *How can I explain this to my father?* he mused. He hoped Customer Service would not share his screw-up with his father, but that was unlikely.

Without even looking at the figures, Spencer knew his decision would now cost the company, and after the last disagreement with his father over how to increase the company's profits, this would be an embarrassment. His father was not one to say *I-told-you-so*, but Spencer felt it, nonetheless.

Spencer tried to take his mind off the problem by watching the lawn maintenance crew hard at work on the spring clean-up, trimming the shrubs and planting the marigold and primrose beds that lined the main entrance of the newest and largest factory building of the three owned by his father's company, CampWild, Inc. On the lawns, the ornamental Eastern Redbuds were beginning to reveal their display of rosy, pink blossoms. His wife liked them so much that he had two of the trees planted on the front lawn at their home.

He could feel the throbbing in his head beginning to subside and his breathing returning to normal.

His intercom buzzed. He returned to his chair and answered.

"Mr. Ward is on line one," said the secretary.

"Did he say what about?" inquired Spencer.

"Negative."

Spencer did not have to guess what it would be about. His father, John, had a knack for catching up to him when it came to his business decisions. Although he had been supervisor of the company's Tenting Division for fourteen and a half years, and had an MBA from Wharton, he still sometimes felt he didn't have the business acumen of his father, who had started the company nearly thirty years ago.

He took a deep breath and pressed the button.

"Yes, Dad?"

"Spencer, good afternoon. My assistant tells me Customer Service reports that there have been several complaints posted online in the last few weeks about zippers breaking on the CT-27 tents we've been shipping out. You need to look into this. If our supplier is sending us defective products, we'll need to set them straight or get a new supplier. Give me their number; I'll make the call."

"Dad, it's okay. I'll take care of it."

"And in the meantime, recall all of the CT-27s made

with the last zipper shipment. I'd rather them not be available than risk bad reviews."

"Not too many have gone out to retail stores yet. The online orders we ship from here, so I have those in the warehouse."

"Alright. Let's keep ahead of this. Say hello to Patty and the kids."

"Bye, Dad."

Spencer sat back in his chair. He didn't have the nerve to tell his father he had changed suppliers to buy zippers at half their usual price. He slammed his fist onto the solid mahogany desk, directing his anger towards the supplier, but in truth, he had to admit his error. He silently berated himself and muttered, *you get what you pay for.*

For years, he had managed to increase profits by finding better deals on components, whether it be the fabrics or grommets, zippers, thread, or cord. He wondered, *have I reached a point where my desire for maximizing profit has become just plain greed?*

His doctor was worried about his increasingly high blood pressure. He reached into the bottom drawer of his desk and pulled out the portable monitor, fastened the cuff around his left bicep, and waited for the results. 160 over 92. *Not good*, he told himself. The doctor had warned that if he wasn't able to make lifestyle changes to keep it down, he would have to go on medication and deal with the side effects. Or he could skip the medication and risk a heart attack. Neither of those options sounded good.

After calming himself with a large glass of water, he made a few calls and had the CT-27s pulled from their online availability. His assistant, Jina Marshall, was put to work notifying the retail stores to pull the tents and wait for return authorizations. He called the floor foreman and had production halted on the CT-27s until he could get a shipment of higher-quality zippers delivered. They also discussed retrofitting the returned tents with the new zippers. It could be done, but it would reduce the profits and put production weeks behind schedule.

Jina suggested, "We could give some overtime and keep the lines running for a couple of hours extra every day until we retrofit all the zippers."

"That would probably be best," Spencer said. "At this point, some profit is better than a big loss."

***

The rest of the afternoon was quiet in the office. On the way out of the building, Spencer stopped in the restroom and looked at himself in the mirror. The bags under his eyes gave him the appearance of a tired old man, even though he had just turned forty-one last month.

This has to change, he thought, *or I won't make it to fifty.*

He turned sideways, straightened his back, and patted his stomach. *I'm not that out of shape,* he told himself. *At least I have my hair.*

"Mr. Ward. Mr. Ward."

He heard his name being called down the hallway. He stepped out of the restroom to see his secretary at the end of the hallway.

"Yes, Brenda. What's up?"

"Your father is on line one."

If it was anyone else calling, Spencer would have told her to have them call back tomorrow, but for his father, he would take the call.

He walked back into his office, set down his briefcase and picked up the phone.

"Yes, Dad?"

"Great, Spencer, you're still here. There's a part-time entry-level opening in the Climbing Division. I know we talked about Jay getting a job now that he's sixteen. It would only be a few hours a week. I don't want him to miss out on being a teen, but developing a sense of work-life is valuable. I wanted to run it by you before I offered it to him."

"It would get him away from the video games for a few hours. He is busy with school and track, though."

"We could work around his schedule until school ends. That's not a problem. He can work more regularly once school's out for the summer."

Spencer ran a quick scenario through his head to see how the discussion would play out at home with Jay. It might not go well. "I'll let him know."

"If you don't mind, Spencer, I'd rather make the offer myself."

Spencer breathed a sigh of relief. "That would be great."

"I know how sixteen-year-old boys and their dads sometimes butt heads. I have experience."

"Don't remind me, Dad."

The two had a laugh and John continued. "Grandpas can work magic. I'll call him tomorrow afternoon."

"Okay, Dad. Have a good weekend."

***

Spencer's son, Jay, shoved his phone back into the back pocket of his jeans and walked into the living room where his father was reading the newspaper in his recliner. At sixteen, Jay was nearly as tall as his father and just as broad-shouldered. His dark hair, brown eyes, and angular nose caused people to often comment that he was a younger version of his father. Spencer felt pride in that, but lately, he got the impression that Jay would rather be seen as his own man.

"That was Grandpa on the phone," Jay said, sitting on the arm of the sofa.

"What did he want?" Spencer folded the paper onto his lap.

"He's offering me a job at CampWild. In the Climbing Division. He said, 'entry-level.'"

"That's great, Jay. Get your foot in the door."

"But doesn't entry-level mean low pay?"

"Yes, but entry-level means there is an opportunity to work your way to a higher level."

Spencer looked at his son. He could sense the unspoken dissatisfaction. This was the argument he was hoping to avoid. *Hopefully,* he thought, *this won't end in a yelling match.*

"Don't think because you are related to the owner, you deserve higher wages. The other employees will resent you for it. Trust me on that."

"Did you get paid better when you started?"

"Not at all. Your grandfather wanted to teach me jobs at every level, starting with the lowest, so that as I got older and higher up in the company, I would understand what is important in each position, from cleaner to line worker to shift supervisor. And now as a division manager, I don't think I would be nearly as good a manager if I hadn't done those other jobs as well."

"How do you know the employees would resent me then if I got paid more?"

"Because someone started a rumor when I was starting at the factory. It wasn't true, of course, but I was treated rather coldly until one day a guy confronted me directly. Next payday, I showed him my paycheck. My hourly rate was the same as his. I made quite a few friends after that."

"Weren't you embarrassed to show them that your family made you work for so little?"

"Yes and no. I was a teenager like you. I wasn't using my paycheck to live on, but I was earning my own money and not having to rely on my parents to dole out cash whenever I wanted to buy something or go to a

movie or whatever. I felt good about that. I think you will, too."

"So, I should say yes? Grandpa told me to think about it and get back to him tomorrow. He will have them hire someone else if I don't want it."

"You didn't tell him no already?"

"He wouldn't let me say either way. He kept saying think about it. I know he wants me to say yes, or he wouldn't have called. Right?"

Spencer was impressed that Jay had the insight to recognize the subtext.

"You can always change your mind later if you decide it's not for you. I'm sure your grandfather will understand."

Spencer hoped his son would stick with it and make his way up the company ladder as he did. *Quitting is not something Wards do.*

Jay asked, "What if I'm no good at the job? What if they fire me?"

"Don't get ahead of yourself. There are many different jobs. Managers move people around to find the position that best suits them. Firing is the last resort. It's something your grandfather insists on, unless you refuse to work. Otherwise, we like to keep employees for a long time."

***

On Saturday morning, Jay hopped into his father's car freshly showered and shaved, wearing a green polo shirt and jeans. Spencer noted Jay's attempt to make a good first impression.

"I hope this is alright," Jay said.

"It's fine, even a T-shirt would be okay in the factory. It's not open to the public."

"Are you working all day? It is Saturday."

"Well, since I'm bringing you to work, I thought I'd take care of a few things while I'm there. I'll meet you at the end of your shift. If you need anything during the day, just call, okay?"

"Sure, Dad."

When they arrived, Spencer dropped his son at the Climbing Division entrance.

"Say hi to Eddie, your supervisor, for me. He'll take good care of you."

Jay looked exasperated. "Do I need to be taken care of?"

"I didn't mean that. He'll get you set, that's all."

Jay closed the car door and Spencer watched him approach the door. *Have a good day*, he thought.

Spencer parked in his designated space and headed into his building. He noticed his father's Mustang in its space. *Odd for Dad to be here on a Saturday. I wonder what's up?*

The building was quiet with no office staff at work. He looked around for his father as he walked down the hall.

It wasn't until he reached his office that he ran into his father.

"Spencer."

"Dad? It's Saturday. Why are you here?"

"I know why you are here. That's why I'm here."

"You're confusing me."

"Your boy needs a ride to work, correct?"

"Yes. And?"

"That means you or Patty have to give him a ride."

"Yes."

"So, I didn't intend his working to interrupt your weekend. I've decided to give Jay a little gift. I have been thinking of buying a new car. I'd like to give Jay the Mustang."

"Dad, I can't let you do that. He's sixteen. Shouldn't he have to save up for a car as I did?"

"We weren't in a position to buy you a car back then. Everything we had was tied up in the company."

"How will he learn responsibility if it's just given to him?"

"Oh, believe me, it comes with strings. Please, Spencer, let an old man spoil his grandson a little."

Dad, you're not old."

"Much older than I want to be. No one is guaranteed a long life."

"You are starting to sound a little morbid."

"Sorry. Anyway, I told Eddie to send Jay over to your office on his break, but we'll meet him at the door. I want to hand him the keys by the car."

"Are you sure about this? That car is practically brand new."

"It's three years old."

***

"He should be out any minute now, Spencer," John said.

"You sound more excited than even Jay will be, Dad."

"I can't help it. I like seeing people be happy."

They stood outside, soaking in the warm sun and enjoying the sweet smell of the blossoms wafting on the soft breeze.

Moments later, Jay emerged from the factory and jogged over to his father and grandfather.

"Am I in trouble already?" asked Jay.

His grandfather laughed. "Has Eddie given you a hard time?"

"Not at all. He's really nice."

That's why I hired him years ago. I like to hire nice people."

Jay stood there looking puzzled, first at his father, then at his grandfather.

"Jay," began his grandfather, "now that you are working, you'll need a way to get back and forth to work without having to pester your parents. Having a license is great but having your own set of wheels is even better."

Spencer watched Jay and imagined the proverbial wheels in his brain spinning.

John held out a set of keys.

"A car?" Jay asked. He looked around the nearly empty parking lot of the office building. "Where?"

"That one," said John, pointing to the Mustang. But before you get too excited, there are conditions."

Jay nodded.

"First, the car stays in my name. It's yours to use. If you get a speeding ticket or any traffic violation, I take the car back for say, three months. Then we try again. Deal?"

"Deal! I promise, no speeding."

"Easier said than done," said Spencer. "Especially when your friends are around."

"Thanks, Grandpa." He gave his grandfather a hug. Spencer was taken aback by Jay's display of affection. It was so unlike him lately.

John handed Jay the keys and turned to Spencer. "Now, son, if I could bum a ride home…"

"Of course, Dad. Give me a few minutes back in my office and I'll be ready to go."

John turned to his grandson. "And you'd better get back. You wouldn't want to get canned on your first day for being late to your post."

"Thanks again, Grandpa." Jay sprinted back to the Climbing Division doorway.

Spencer watched his son as he ran and tried to remember his excitement about getting his first car.

He turned to his father, about to thank him when he saw his father grimacing and pressing his abdomen.

"Are you okay, Dad?"

"Yeah, I think it's just a little indigestion."

Spencer looked at his father closely. He never noticed before, but his father was looking older and frailer. *Maybe it's just the light,* he told himself.

CHAPTER 2

Changes

Jay settled into his job at the factory and even asked for more hours. Spencer's daughter, Rachel, was off to music camp for July, and Patty kept herself busy with volunteering for their church and the local food pantry. *It's just as well,* thought Spencer. They didn't seem to have much to talk about these days except the necessary running-of-the-household discussions.

Spencer found himself staring out of his office window toward the drifting cumulus clouds without noticing them. From his subconsciousness, the same questions arose as they had for the past couple of years. *Is this all there is to my life? I feel like I should be happy, so what is missing? What needs to change?*

The answers never seemed to materialize. Spencer sighed and sat up at his desk, refocusing on his stack of orders and invoices. Thinking about life was hard. It seemed easier to be busy with work.

Now that summer was here, CampWild expected an influx of last-minute orders from retail outlets that underestimated sales and were now caught short. All of the faulty tent zippers had been replaced and the Tenting Division was fully prepared for the summer rush. *At least I'm good at my job,* he thought.

"Your father is on line one," Spencer's secretary said over the intercom.

Spencer pressed the button. "What's up, Dad?"

"I need to see you at four. Try to wrap up by then. Meet me at my office. I'll explain when you get here." He hung up before Spencer had a chance to respond.

That's odd, thought Spencer. He looked at his clock: 2:30.

His younger brother, Ronan, was head of the Camping Division, where all of the camping gear, except for the tents and dining flies, were produced. After hesitating several times, he decided to give his brother a call. Either he wasn't summoned to their father's office, or he was, and if he was, he might know why.

"Yeah, Dad called me, too," answered Ronan. "But I have no idea why either."

"He's been acting a little odd lately, not that I've seen him much."

"You don't think he's losing it, do you?"

"No, not odd like that. I can't figure it out. Well, see you at four."

Spencer disconnected, then made a few calls, leaving himself a note reminding himself of tomorrow's important tasks.

***

Ronan entered the lobby as Spencer was stepping into the elevator.

"Hold up," called Ronan. He jogged to the elevator.

"Thanks, bro," he said, a little out of breath. "Not all of us have a cushy office in the main HQ."

"It's only because my division is right next door. I didn't build the camping building where it is. Blame Dad, not me."

"Just busting your chops, big brother."

The elevator reached the third floor and the two brothers stepped out. Their father's secretary smiled and waved them into his office.

"Hello, boys."

"You'll never stop calling us boys, will you Dad?" asked Ronan. "Spencer's forty-one and I'm turning thirty-five. We haven't been boys for a while now."

"You'll always be my boys."

Spencer laughed, but then he noticed his father's eyes were getting glassy like he was holding back tears.

"You'll always be my boys," John repeated. He looked out his large office window and seemed lost in thought.

"Dad?" Spencer asked.

"I have something I need to tell you both. It's not easy for me to say. So, I'll just put it out there. I have pancreatic cancer. Stage four."

The room was silent as the two brothers took in the news.

"But you can get treatments, right? Chemo or radiation or something?" asked Ronan.

"We're beyond that."

"What do you mean, Dad?" Spencer asked.

"I've done all that, it's over."

"How long have you known?" Ronan asked with a bit of an edge to his voice.

"About two years."

"Two years!" both brothers exclaimed in unison.

"Why didn't you tell us?" Spencer asked. He couldn't find the emotion he needed to feel. He was part angry, part sad, and part scared for his father, for their family, and for the business.

"I didn't want to worry you. I thought I could beat it and continue on as usual."

"Does Mom know?"

"Yes, but I swore her to secrecy. She has helped me through all of the treatments, appointments, and medications. Your mother is a saint. Saint Roslyn. Has a nice ring to it."

"What about Tina? Does she know?"

"I got off the phone with your sister just before you came in. I didn't want her calling you with the news before I got the chance to tell you myself. You know Tina. She never could keep a secret."

"So, what happens now?"

"Well, I'm still here. We'll take it one day at a time. The doctor says I could have up to a year before…" he trailed off. "There's a lot I could get done in a year. A lot of good. But before you go worrying about the company, here's my idea: Spencer will take my place here. Ronan, you have a choice. Take Spencer's position as head of Tenting or stay where you are in Camping. I know you have said how much you like your work there."

Spencer took the opportunity to lighten the mood. "Stay where you are or get a cushy office in HQ. Tough choice, bro."

Ronan was quick to respond. "I'll stay where I am. To be honest, I'm thinking of proposing to Beth, and taking on a new division right now would make my head swim."

"Beth is a lovely girl, Ronan. I've seen you two together for a while now. I think you two will be very happy."

"Thanks, Dad. That means a lot."

"One very important thing," John continued, "I don't want this to get out about my illness. Please, the fewer people that know, the better as far as I'm concerned."

Spencer already decided not to tell his family right away. His wife would want her ladies' prayer circle to pray for him and they would all know, and almost assuredly there would be gossip among them. His kids didn't need to feel guilty for enjoying their teen activities when Grandpa is sick. He would make a point of having them visit their grandparents often, though.

"We'll do whatever you want, Dad. If you need anything, we're always available. Or if Mom needs help, tell her not to be a saint and call us."

John stood up and walked around to the front of his desk and pulled his two sons close.

The moment was interrupted by Spencer's phone buzzing in his pocket.

"Sorry," he said, pulling out his phone.

He looked down at the Caller ID: "It's Tina."

The three men laughed and hugged again. Spencer closed his eyes, wanting to remember this feeling. For this moment, all of their business disagreements and head-butting didn't mean anything.

***

The next few days were a numbing kind of awareness for Spencer. He kept on with his regular schedule, fully cognizant of the changes on the horizon. He found it surprisingly easy to keep the information from his wife. It had been a long time since they'd confided in each other, content with the day-to-day minutiae that passed for a relationship.

Work presented more immediate concerns. Spencer wanted to prepare Jina, his assistant, for her promotion but needed to keep the promise to his father. *It's lucky I can rely on her to take care of so many details*, he mused. *She probably knows this division better than I do.*

When he heard her return to her desk after her lunch break, he called her into his office for a run-down of the afternoon's necessary business.

"Sorry I'm a little late, your father asked me to meet with him."

"Really? What about?" Spencer's curiosity was aroused.

"He asked me how I liked working for you. How I liked the Tenting Division. Where I see myself in five years. It was a little odd, I must say. I felt like I was being interviewed." Jina gave a slight laugh. "I said that to him."

"What did he say to that?"

"First, he wanted me to answer his questions, which I did. I like working here, for you, and the company has been very good to me."

"Even when I've lost my temper and yelled at you?"

"It's been a while since those days."

"So, what did he say about the interview question?"

"He said he's looking ahead to possibly retiring in a few years or sooner. And if you were to take over the company, did I think I could handle running the Tenting Division."

"You would be the perfect person to run this division, Jina. I would support that one hundred percent."

"Mr. Ward. You are making me blush."

"I will let him know you have my support and recommendation."

"Thank you, Mr. Ward. But it's a far distant possibility. In the meantime, you called me in to discuss today's tasks."

They set about going over the clients to contact, bills to send, and supplies to order. In the back of his mind,

Spencer was relieved that his father had taken care of addressing Jina's promotion. How easily his father handled the situation without a hint of his illness.

His illness.

Contrary to what his father told Jina, retirement in a few years was a dream. According to what Spencer had read, Pancreatic cancer was a certain death sentence, even with today's medical capabilities. It is rare for a person to live three years after diagnosis, and John was already beyond two.

Spencer's phone buzzed.

"Your father is on line one."

He picked up the receiver. "Yes, Dad?"

"Don't forget to stop by the house on your way home. I've got some things to give you and some to give your brother before your sister gets here from Portland."

"I won't forget. See you later."

After the call was over, Spencer caught his breath. *When will it be the last time I say that? How soon will there be no more later?*

***

When Spencer arrived at his parents' house, the house he and his siblings grew up in, Ronan hadn't arrived. His father was waiting on the porch, patting the seat next to his for Spencer to sit down.

"It's time we had the talk, Spencer."

"Dad, it's a little late for the puberty talk."

"Probably," his father said, chuckling. "This is a little more serious."

Spencer inhaled and let out his breath slowly. "I know."

"I've known you for a long time, son. I've watched you do some great things, and I've watched you make some big mistakes. You have a bit of a temper, always have had since you were a small boy. You like to win. Losing was always hard for you to accept. People were hard for you to accept."

Spencer opened his mouth to protest.

"Let me finish. The world is full of people just trying to make their way. Like you, they may do great things, or they may screw up badly. Sometimes they hurt you, intentionally or not. It's been my experience to try to see the good in people. Sometimes you win them over, but not always. What I'm getting at is try not to shut yourself off from people."

"I don't," protested Spencer.

"How are things with Patty?"

Spencer recoiled. "Fine."

"Are they? I think things could be better from what I see. But it's your life. I'm suggesting you could be happier if you try to be more accepting of people. Nobody's perfect. I have found the more I show kindness, the more compassionate I am toward others, and the happier I am. I've had a happy life. Yes, I've been successful in business,

but I'm more pleased that I have been happy. That's what I hope for you, Ronan, and Tina."

Ronan's Jeep pulled into the driveway.

"I thought you said six," Ronan said, looking at his watch. "It's ten of. Did I miss anything?"

"No," John said, "we were just chatting. Follow me to the garage."

John reached into the entry door and pressed the button to raise the large garage door.

"I know your sister won't be interested in any of this stuff, so help yourselves to it."

John pointed to several boxes of old sporting equipment and fishing poles.

"This feels weird, Dad," Ronan said.

"Getting presents from your father?"

"You know what I mean."

"Giving people gifts makes me happy. And I like being happy. So, make me happy and take this stuff. Make yourself happy."

"Got it, Dad," Ronan said. "Happy."

John proceeded to recount stories for each item and time went by barely noticed by the three men. After a while, Roslyn called out to the garage that dinner was ready.

"I'd better be going," said Spencer.

"Nonsense. Your mother called Patty this afternoon and told her you'd be having dinner with us."

"Nobody told Beth. But I can text her. She won't mind. I don't want to miss Mom's cooking."

"Don't tell Beth that," John joked.

***

In the next two weeks, John's health took a rapid turn. He stopped coming in to work, and Spencer began spending more time in his father's office taking care of necessary business. Tina had flown in from Portland and was staying with their parents, trying to stay out of the way of the nurses who kept a close eye on John's condition.

"There is not a lot we can do except make him comfortable," explained one of the nurses.

Tina sat with him, looking through old photo albums and between them, remembering details of family trips and celebrations.

One evening, John asked the nurse on duty to help him to the back porch where he could watch the sunset with Roslyn. He carried the photo album he had been looking at, the album of the kids when they were little.

When Roslyn joined him in the wicker chair next to his, they looked through the album together until the sun touched the horizon.

"We did well, dear," John said. "We raised some really great kids."

"That we did."

"And we did some good for others along the way."

"That we did, too."

"I wish I could do more," John said.

"You will."

Roslyn took his hand and they watched in silence as the oranges and purples grew dimmer and the lightning bugs began to blink above the lawn.

The photo album slipped from John's lap and hit the porch floor with a thud that startled Roslyn.

She turned to John. His hand still felt warm, but she knew.

"I love you, John," she whispered. She turned back to the sunset and watched until the last color faded from the sky.

CHAPTER 3

Stories

Spencer Ward looked again into the open casket. He recognized the tie his father was wearing. A royal blue with silver threads in a crisscross pattern. A Father's Day gift from the three of them when they were kids. *I'll bet he chose to be buried in that.*

Spencer took a deep breath and exhaled with slow, measured control. The scent from the numerous flower arrangements added an unexpected note of sweetness to his grief. Tasteful wreaths and bouquets of lilies, large sprays of gladioli, and rose arrangements of yellow and white were placed along the walls under soft spotlights. His mother insisted on the lavender and white arrangement for the casket, lavender being John's favorite color.

You would have loved the flowers, Dad, Spencer thought.

The carpet muffled the sound of his brother, Ronan, approaching. His brother placed a hand on his shoulder. "Mom and Tina are here."

"Good. How's Mom doing?"

"Surprisingly well. I think she and Dad had a long time to say goodbye and settle their affairs. Tina said she and Mom had a good time yesterday going through old photo albums to put together the display." Ronan paused. "How are you doing?"

Spencer looked his brother in the eyes. "Okay, I

guess. Not sure I'm ready to be in charge of the company, but it is what it is."

"You'll do great. You know I'll have your back."

"Thanks. Just look at all of these flowers."

"Who are they from?" Ronan opened a tag. 'Condolences. The Richards.' They are former neighbors, I think."

Spencer opened one. 'Sorry for your loss. Morgan Outdoors.' Oh, they are a customer, a big client."

"They just put in a large order for camping gear."

Spencer tipped his head toward his father's casket. "We probably shouldn't be talking business now."

"I don't see why not. CampWild was Dad's baby. He'd be happy we're keeping it going."

They continued down the row of arrangements, reading aloud each card or tag.

"You were a popular guy, Dad," Ronan said after reading a dozen complimentary cards.

"Here's one," said Spencer. 'Thank you, John. Although you would never admit it, I know you were the one to fund the new playground at McKinley Park.' "It's not signed."

"Did he fund the playground?" asked Ronan.

"I have no idea."

The funeral director cleared his throat softly from the visitation room doorway and tapped his wrist. "It's time. The guests are beginning to arrive."

Spencer nodded and retreated around the corner of the L-shaped room. He motioned for his family to join them. The video screen they were viewing was scrolling through photos of John while Moonlight Sonata played. Spencer was momentarily taken back to an image of his father sitting in his easy chair, eyes closed, listening to this, one of his favorite Beethoven pieces. He glanced toward the open casket and imagined his father just resting there, listening even now.

As Roslyn passed the display table, she adjusted the arrangement of John's fishing trophies, moving them back from the photo albums and business awards.

The funeral director was warm and pleasant, but matter of fact. He guided Roslyn to the head of the receiving line, followed by Spencer and Patty, Ronan and Tina, and finally the teens, Jay and Rachel, who stood nearest the exit to the lobby. This arrangement would allow visitors to pay their respects without lingering too long.

Spencer heard the first of the guests being greeted by the funeral director and being asked to sign the register. He hoped he could recognize everyone in the dimly lit room.

Rachel approached her father. "What if I don't know the people? What do I say?"

"Thank them for coming. If they don't tell you first, you could ask them how they knew your grandfather."

Rachel took her place in line as the first visitors entered the room. An elderly woman, escorted by an aide, approached.

"Mrs. Klafter, so nice to see you," said Spencer. "It's been a while."

"Your mother keeps me informed." She reached out and patted Roslyn's arm. "Your parents are so proud of you kids."

"That we are," Roslyn agreed.

"It's very sad about John." She reached out to hug Spencer, and he stepped forward to steady her as she squeezed him. She then proceeded down the line with kind words for everyone.

A steady stream of well-wishers flowed through the room and offered condolences or shared a brief memory of John. Spencer could see his mother's eyes sparkle when she smiled.

"Your father was a good man," she whispered to Spencer between well-wishers. "I know it, but it's comforting to hear it from others."

Instead of feeling sad, which Spencer had fully expected, he found himself sharing his mother's high spirits as stories were shared.

Two women approached.

"Laura Pearson. And this is my daughter, Stephanie." She shook hands with Roslyn, Spencer, and Patty. "John was such a dear and a wonderful employer. His gift was such a blessing to our family."

"His gift?" Spencer asked.

"Oh, yes. You see, Stephanie was very sick and missed the deadline for a scholarship application.

Without it, we couldn't afford for Stephanie to go to the college with the program she wanted. When John found out, he gave us the same amount as the scholarship would have been and then some. Stephanie is now finishing up her schooling in veterinary medicine. We're so proud of her and so thankful to John."

Roslyn took Stephanie's hand. "You take good care of those animals. John always loved his pets."

"Thank you, Mrs. Ward," Stephanie said. "I will."

The two moved along, and Spencer leaned in toward his mother.

"What's the deal with Dad giving her that money? That seems so generous."

"Your dad liked being generous. And he liked animals too. I'll tell you more later."

Spencer made a mental note to remind his mother.

Patty whispered, "I had no idea there would be this many people. Old and young. It's like half the town is here."

"We are the town's biggest employer, and Dad's been around for a long time."

"There's got to be more to it than that."

Spencer didn't want to get into speculating. He glanced down the receiving line. "Jay and Rachel seem to be doing just fine."

Patty looked down the line as Rachel looked up. They gave each other a little wave.

Spencer finished shaking hands with one of his

parents' neighbors and turned back toward his mother. When he looked up, he recognized the face of the approaching man immediately. Russell Biggs, an employee Spencer fired a few years ago. He remembered the scene. Russell refused to attend an important sales conference in Oakland for family reasons and at that time, Spencer gave him an ultimatum—go or be fired.

Russell gave his condolences to Roslyn and reached out to shake Spencer's hand.

"Spencer, long time."

"Yes," Spencer replied, having a hard time coming up with more to say.

"Sorry about your dad. A great guy."

"Yes," he repeated. "I know you must hate me for letting you go."

"We each did what we thought was best at the time. My daughter needed me, and family comes first in my book. Besides, I see CampWild is doing well without me."

"Yes, it is."

Russell continued. "In the long run, firing me was the best thing you could have done for me. It gave me time to reevaluate my career priorities and decide what to do to move forward. Your dad helped me through the process and sent me commissions on accounts I'd landed for the company. Then he gave me the seed money to start my motorcycle shop with the stipulation that if it became successful, I'd help someone else. I'm happy to say that I have three shops now, Bigg's Bikes, with eighteen employees. I've also helped my cousin to open a second-hand clothing consignment shop, something she'd always dreamed of doing."

"That's great," Spencer responded, but he knew no commissions are paid after an employee leaves the company. And he certainly knew no commissions were paid to Russell out of his division's budget. *What did Dad do that for?* Spencer wondered. *And why?*

Even though the room was full, there was a lull in people waiting to speak to the family, so Spencer took the opportunity to visit the restroom. On his way, he caught a snippet of conversation between two middle-aged women he did not recognize from behind.

"I heard from Henrietta that Mr. Ward was the anonymous donor to the library renovation fund."

"How does she know?"

"The man who brought the money works for Mr. Ward."

"Oh. Interesting."

Spencer continued across the room.

". . . and he paid her hospital bill. The whole thing," said a tall man in a gray suit.

"Let's face it, he could afford it," a shorter man responded.

"True, but it was generous of him."

Spencer assumed the conversation was about his father, but he was a little upset that he had never heard of these things.

***

After the brief graveside service, in accordance with their father's wishes not to have an elaborate ceremony, the family and a few close friends and neighbors returned to the Ward home for a meal prepared and delivered by well-wishers. Everyone pitched in to set the table and set out the mid-afternoon luncheon. There was plenty to choose from: zucchini lasagna (John's favorite), baked ziti, loaves of bread, rolls, cold cuts and cheeses, and a variety of salads and desserts. Spencer's kids took their dad's suggestion to eat out on the back deck away from the adults.

Inside, one of the Ward's long-time neighbors chatted with Roslyn.

"I've always been curious, Roslyn, why you and John stayed in this house. John could have bought or built the nicest house in the neighborhood."

"But this was our home, where we raised our children. John was sentimental in that way. And I am too, I suppose. I don't want to move, even now."

Spencer moved in closer when he noticed his mother's eyes welling up. "We had everything we needed right here. Right, Mom? Dad never believed in ostentatious displays. No mansions or Maseratis for him."

"He always said wherever his family lived would be the best home for him. A castle or a hovel, as long as the family was there."

"I'd draw the line at hovel, myself," added Tina, joining the conversation.

"Dad worked too hard for that ever to happen," Spencer replied.

***

When the last of the guests departed, Tina filled a tray with glasses of leftover lemonade and distributed them to the family settled into the living room.

"So, Tina, no kids or hubby this trip?" asked Spencer.

"A toddler and a seven-year-old would not mix with a funeral. It was hard enough just making arrangements for me to make the trip. Besides, I want the kids to remember their grandpa the way he was when they saw him last month, laughing and having fun with them."

"That was John," Roslyn said. "He never let his pain get in the way of his work or his fun."

Spencer swallowed a lump in his throat. "That's the way we'll all remember Dad. I was always amazed that he never seemed to get angry, no matter how bad things got messed up at work."

"We'll manage, he used to say," added Ronan. "And he always did."

Silence followed as everyone seemed absorbed in their own memories. Spencer wondered if he would be able to manage crises at work without losing his temper now that he would have the stress of a higher position. *How did Dad do that?*

Roslyn sat quietly, her eyes welling.

"I'm sorry, Mom," Spencer said. "I didn't mean to upset you."

"It's not that, Spencer. I'm not upset. I am just remembering how your father and I spent these last few weeks. He wanted to go through our photo albums. All of them, in order, like he was reliving his life story. We had so many laughs. You kids gave us a lot to laugh about."

"Like what, Mom?" asked Tina.

"There are so many. One your father was particularly tickled by was when Spencer was five, he got into your father's closet and dressed up in his white shirt, tie, and suit. Then he clomped around the house in his father's dress shoes, dragging his heavy briefcase, and announcing to everyone that he was off to work to make a million dollars."

"And in my defense, I've done it, I might add," Spencer said.

"It took a few years, though," Ronan teased.

"It pays to have goals."

Tina started laughing. "I remember when Ronan ran through the house holding the end of the toilet paper and pulling a long stream behind him."

Ronan blushed. "I was probably two."

"Two and a half," Spencer teased. "Old enough to know better."

They all laughed at the memory. Spencer was glad to see his mother in a good mood.

"I remember I was mad when Dad made us spend a

Saturday picking up trash on the roadside," said Spencer. "Dad said he would rather spend a day cleaning up the trash than getting upset every time he drove by it. I didn't get it then, but now I do."

Ronan added, "Remember the summer he made us mow Mrs. Klafter's lawn after she broke her hip? And he wouldn't let her pay us?"

"Yes, but she did bake us cookies," Spencer said.

"Which Mom made us share with Tina." Ronan gave Tina a look and she stuck her tongue out at him in return.

"What are you, twelve?" Ronan asked. "That's a memory I'd like to forget. My sister in middle school. You were such a—"

Their mother interrupted. "Your father was trying to teach you boys to be helpful to those in need."

"Yes, Mom. We know," Ronan said. "But at fourteen, it doesn't always sink in right away."

"That's why they say you live and learn," Roslyn added.

"I want to hear a story about you and Dad," Tina prodded.

Roslyn thought for a minute, then a smile lit up her face. "This is a funny one. We were on vacation in New Orleans before you kids were born, staying at a fancy hotel. The company was starting to do well, and we decided it was time for a vacation. There was a young newlywed couple we met whose luggage was misplaced at the airport, so they had nothing but the clothes they

were wearing. Your father suggested we take them shopping and buy them a few things. Your dad took the groom to a men's shop for items, and I took the bride shopping. While we were out, and the groom was trying on clothes, your father called a flower shop and ordered six dozen red roses to be delivered to their room at the hotel, three dozen signed from the groom to the bride and three dozen signed from the bride to the groom. When we got back to the hotel, we helped them carry their things to their room. Can you imagine their looks of surprise? When they read the tags, they didn't know what to think. And of course, we claimed to have no idea."

"You two were a little naughty in your day, Mom," said Tina. "You didn't get me six dozen roses when I got married."

"I didn't give that couple roses either. Technically, your father did. It was his idea."

The conversation paused as if there was a sudden realization of the reason they were gathered there.

"I miss him," said Tina, hugging a small throw pillow.

Roslyn took a sip of her lemonade and held the glass between her hands as if in prayer. "Your father was sad to go. There was so much more he wanted to do."

"We saw on one of the flower cards that someone thought Dad had funded the new playground at McKinley Park. Did he?" Spencer asked his mother.

"No one was supposed to know, but yes, he did. This was a few years ago. The old one was in bad shape and the town didn't have it in the budget for new swings or whatever. Your Dad saw the board meeting write-up in the paper."

"How much did that set him back?"

"That I don't know. I don't think it mattered. He just wanted to do something nice for the town."

Nice comes with a price, Spencer thought. *I wonder what else he's funded.*

CHAPTER 4

New Beginnings

S pencer pulled his BMW into the CampWild main parking lot as usual and swung the car into his space without thinking. He shut off the engine and opened the door. It was then he realized he should be parking in the space next to the entrance where his father always parked. The RESERVED FOR MR. WARD sign still applied, so he restarted the car and changed spaces.

He stepped out of his car and took a moment to look over the building in front of him. Three stories of alternating layers of green panels and windows rose from the highest ground on the property. Although the building itself was not immense in width or length, its height made it seem more impressive. The bright red CampWild name and tent logo mounted along the top of the building could be seen from the highway about a quarter mile away. Spencer remembered when his father had to be convinced to spend the extra money for the oversized sign.

"Endless advertising to every car that passes by," Spencer said, trying to get him to agree. "It will pay for itself over time."

When his father wavered, Spencer reminded him,

"You sent me to Wharton to get my MBA. This is the kind of thing I learned."

The memory made Spencer smile. He stepped up to the entry door, which slid open as he approached.

"Good morning, Mr. Ward," the receptionist said.

"Morning," Spencer replied, nodding his head in her direction. He took the elevator to the top floor and walked down the hall to his father's, now his, office.

The door to his outer office already had a new nameplate. Spencer Ward, CEO.

Dad must have ordered that, he thought. *Thanks, Dad.*

His secretary had not arrived yet, and he was glad he would have a few minutes to himself to get acclimated. He walked past the secretary's desk and into his office. He closed the door and switched on the light.

He was glad his father had taken the time to go over many of the company operations in preparation. Never expecting to be in charge so soon, Spencer wished he had absorbed more of what his father was telling him. *Too late now,* he told himself. *Sink or swim.* He knew that was not entirely accurate. His father had two long-time assistants who ran many of the day-to-day operations, as John directed. Spencer knew them somewhat but expected to be working closely with them now.

He heard a soft knocking on the door.

"Come in," he said.

"Good morning, Mr. Ward."

"Good morning, Gracie."

"Is there anything you need?"

"I'll be sure to let you know. Oh, when Steve and Roger get in, could you have them come to my office?"

"Sure. They should be in soon."

"Great."

Gracie closed the door behind her as she stepped into the outer office.

A couple of minutes later, the intercom buzzed.

"Your brother is on line two," Gracie announced.

Spencer pressed the button.

"Yes, Ronan. What is it?"

"Well, now that you are the big cheese," Ronan teased, "I need to know if you've checked out the executive bathroom yet?"

"No. But you are welcome to come have a look."

"Maybe later. I was calling to wish you good luck on your first day."

"Thanks, brother. It feels very weird to be in Dad's office at Dad's desk."

"It's yours now."

"I know. I know. I will get used to it."

"Well, I'll let you go. Oh, one last thing . . . could I have a raise?"

"Goodbye, Ronan. Nice try."

Spencer leaned back in the high-backed office chair, feeling at once comfortable and anxious. He opened his briefcase and picked up the bottle of ibuprofen. *Two ought to do.*

A few minutes later he heard a light knock on his door.

"Come in."

Steve and Roger entered. Neither was wearing a suit jacket, but looked sharp enough in dress shirts and ties. Both had worked for Spencer's father for as long as he could remember, though he wasn't exactly sure what their roles were in the company. They each held the title of Assistant to Mr. Ward. He gestured toward two chairs in front of the large, mahogany desk. The men sat down. Steve had a smile on his face as usual. His round face with rosy cheeks always seemed to project inner happiness. *No wonder Dad liked to have him around,* Spencer thought.

Roger was a milder personality. He always seemed to be contemplating something serious. That was Spencer's first thought when he met him years ago, and that impression had never changed. Not that he was unfriendly, but it was hard to know what Roger was thinking behind those thick glasses.

Steve spoke first: "To avoid being awkward, how would you like us to address you?"

At first, Spencer wasn't sure what Steve meant. The puzzled look on his face prompted Steve to elaborate.

"Mr. Ward? Spencer?"

"Spencer would be fine. That's what you've always called me."

"But you weren't the boss then."

"What did you call Dad?"

"John, when we were in-house, but if clients were present, always Mr. Ward."

"I like the sound of that. Let's do that." Spencer hesitated. He knew the sooner he brought up the subject, the less awkward it would be. "You two have been around for a long time and probably know the workings of the company better than I do. But . . . " he paused. The two men looked at him wide-eyed. "I'm not sure exactly what your roles are in the company."

Steve, the older and somewhat heavier of the two employees, moved toward the edge of his chair. "I'm responsible for sales and expenditure analysis. And anything else Mr. Ward, uh, your father, needed me to do."

"And I work with personnel and plant operations, plus anything else Mr. Ward needed me to do," added Roger.

"I'd like you to continue as you are, but write up your job descriptions, the kinds of things you've done for my father, so I know who to call on with similar tasks. I'm hoping there are no hiccups in the transition."

"Just as your father would have wanted," said Roger.

There was a moment of awkward silence. Steve and Roger glanced at each other.

"Is there something else?" asked Spencer.

"I guess, well, we should ask if the anonymous gifts will continue."

"Anonymous gifts?" asked Spencer.

The two men looked at each other again.

"You aren't aware?" asked Steve.

Spencer shook his head.

"Your father was a very generous man. Whenever he heard of a person or group that needed financial assistance, he would dispatch one of us to deliver a gift anonymously. Sometimes it was helping someone with rent, or a hospital bill," explained Steve.

"Or donating to a charity or youth group. He once paid for a high school French class to go to Quebec for a long weekend."

"Then there was the new library building."

"How much are we talking?" Spencer asked. "All together."

"A lot," they both said in unison.

"Thousands? Millions?"

"Over the years," Steve mused, "probably more like millions. He's been doing this a long time. That's how I ended up here working for him."

Spencer waited for Steve to continue.

"I was working for Greystone Manufacturing about twenty-five years ago. Part of my job was to climb the catwalk above the furnaces and read the gauges hourly. Of course, that's all done by computer now. Well, one of the furnaces was way out of whack and before I could get out of the way, it exploded, sending me flying off the catwalk and onto the factory floor. My leg was mangled. I had a concussion and a dislocated shoulder.

"I remember waking up at the hospital with my wife and your father next to my bed. John said he told the hospital staff he was my brother. I had no idea who he was, and I thought I must have had amnesia. My wife then explained that your dad was a customer at the bank where she was a teller. He said he was there to help if he could. Every day he would stop by the hospital and check on my recovery. Unfortunately, the doctors could not save my leg and it was amputated at the knee." Steve lifted his pant leg to show the artificial limb.

"I couldn't go back to my factory job. John told me when I was well enough, I was to call him, and he would find me a job. But I thought if I couldn't work at the Greystone plant, how was I going to work at the CampWild facilities? So, I didn't call. And when your dad called me a couple of times a month, I wouldn't answer. I didn't want to let him down."

Roger interjected, shaking his head, "We didn't know that wasn't possible with your dad."

"One day, he showed up at my house and insisted my wife let him in to speak to me. When I tried to explain that I would be no good to him, he asked me if I could answer the telephone. I said yes. He said then there is a job for me at CampWild. And here I am, twenty-four years later. He even paid for me to take courses at the community college to get my associate degree in finance."

"I never knew any of this. I'm so glad it worked out for you," Spencer said, still taking in the enormity of the story. He looked at Roger.

"My turn?" Roger joked. "Well, my story isn't as dramatic as Steve's, but the result is the same. I'm here."

"So, what's the story?" asked Spencer. It fascinated him to learn all of this about his father.

"It was after work, December 17, and getting dark. I had just picked up my two little boys from the sitter and was on my way home. I hit a patch of ice, and my car spun out of control, right into a snow-filled ravine. Luckily, no one was injured, but the boys were scared and wailing. I couldn't calm them down. There were no nearby houses, and it was biting cold. I was thinking, should I try to walk somewhere with the boys or stay in the car? I couldn't get a signal on my flip phone so far out of town, so I stayed in the car with the boys now in my lap.

"It seemed like forever, getting darker and colder. I saw the lights of a car approaching, so I sat the boys in the seat beside me and climbed out and up the embankment waving my arms. Your Dad drove up. I had no idea who he was at the time, just a stranger willing to help a stranded dad and his kids. He helped me load the boys and their car seats into his back seat and gave us a ride. I said to the nearest house, but he insisted on driving us home. He thought the boys had been through enough, which was true.

"On the ride, he asked me about my life, where I worked, and about my family. He told me not to worry about the car, he'd call a tow truck. I told him I would take care of it, but he insisted. Five days later, I looked out my window and there was my car, all repaired, not a dent on it."

"How did you end up working here?"

"That's the thing. The department store where I was a checkout clerk was about to lay off some people. I figured it was going to be me because I had to call out for a few days because of my broken car. Somehow your dad knew. He called me and offered me a job at the warehouse at more than I was making at the store. Of course, I accepted. There was one condition, though: I had to take business classes at the college, but he would pay. After I got my degree, he promoted me to his assistant. He told my wife he would pay her tuition as well, and she recently got her cosmetology license. We are so much better off now than before we met your dad. And it all started because of a chance meeting on an icy road."

"Wow," Spencer said. "Incredible." His mind was racing. *How did I not know any of this?*

"He swore us to secrecy. He didn't want anyone to know of his good deeds. He didn't want any recognition," explained Steve.

"He said that seeing people live better lives or experience joy is what made him happy," added Roger. "And I was glad to help."

"I'll admit, it wasn't always easy to give gifts anonymously," said Steve.

"What do you mean?" asked Spencer. "I would think it would be easy."

"Let me tell you about my first time. After your father hired me, and I was still getting used to my prosthetic leg, he said he had a small job for me. I was to go to a house, the green one on Academy Street, and tell them an anonymous donor would be paying for a new roof. They didn't believe me, saying I was playing a cruel joke. I assured them I wasn't, and all they had to do was pick out the shingles. They did, finally. I hired a roofing company, and they got their new roof. They even tried to get the roofers to say who hired them, but since the roofers only knew of me, the homeowners never found out."

"Do you know why my dad picked their house? I'm sure there were many houses that could have used a new roof."

"I'm not sure how he knew, but the guy who lives there was a disabled veteran," said Steve.

"Your dad was a keen listener. He always had an ear out for a chance to help someone," Roger explained. "He sometimes visited the employee lunchrooms to chat. He might hear something there. But he also listened in stores, on the sidewalks, and even in the bank. He created his own opportunities."

"So that's why I asked if the anonymous gifts would continue."

"Let's put that on hold for now. I need to get a better handle on the company's financial situation. Steve, let's meet this afternoon and you can fill me in on that. Dad always painted a sunny picture no matter what state the company was in."

"When you were a boy, the company almost went under," Steve said. "But we pulled through."

"Let's hope it doesn't come to that again," said Spencer.

CHAPTER 5

Stress

"How did I not know this?" Spencer asked, looking over the figures Roger had brought in for their afternoon meeting. The charts all seemed to be trending downward, and the financial reports were similarly dismal. He could feel his blood pressure rising and another headache coming on. *Calm down*, he told himself. *Breathe.*

"Your father's original patents ended a couple of years ago," Roger explained. "We've been losing ground since cheaper knockoffs have been flooding the market. Our development team hasn't come up with patentable products lately, and we have a few more patents set to expire within a year or two."

"So we'll be in worse shape than we are now?" Spencer asked.

"Well, maybe Sales and Marketing would have some ideas. Your father was pretty set in his ideas for sales, but in the last few years, the marketplace has been changing. Sales conferences have their place, but as you can see here, a larger share of our sales are now online, and brick-and-mortar orders are stagnant, even declining in some areas."

"Alright, set up a meeting with Sales. Let's try to get ahead of this."

"Will do." Roger left the office. Spencer reached for his ibuprofen, now handy in the desk's top side drawer.

Spencer had not yet explored the contents of the desk's other side drawers. He pulled open the bottom drawer and lifted the contents, a stack of papers and envelopes, onto the desk in front of him.

One by one, he read the pages. Thank you notes from customers and wholesale contacts.

This must be his feel-good collection, thought Spencer. Words like superior and quality, outstanding and generous appeared frequently. Letters were dated from the early days of the company until recently, all positive and glowing. *No wonder the company grew so quickly.*

One letter stood out from the others. Not typical of business correspondence, it was in a pink envelope with the company's address in neat penmanship, not typed like the others. Spencer's curiosity was piqued.

He read quickly, amazed at the contents. His father had given a grieving mother money for funeral expenses when her young son died unexpectedly. She had no money for a funeral or burial and his father's gift meant her son would have a respectable ceremony. He had even purchased a headstone. The last sentence of her letter hit home: *I wish good health for you and your family, and I hope as a parent you never have to experience the loss of a child.*

Spencer looked at the letter's postmark. He would

have been eight years old when this happened. He tried to imagine his father's reaction to this woman's grief. *How would Dad have felt about losing Ronan, Tina, or me?* Spencer's chest felt heavy thinking about his own children, Jay and Rachel. *Worrying about your kids is one thing, but losing a child must be devastating.*

He shook his head to clear his thoughts, took a deep breath, and wiped a tear from his eye. *Back to work,* he said to himself. *The rest of these can wait for another day.* He set the stack back into the drawer.

He re-examined the charts and figures Roger had left. No division was doing great, though Ronan's was doing better than the others. *No wonder he wanted to stay there.*

Either we increase income or decrease expenses, or both. He remembered the zipper debacle that cost his division quite a bit in lost revenue. *One wrong decision, big consequences. And that was at the division level. Company-level decisions would mean bigger consequences.* That thought didn't make it easier to move forward.

***

The head of sales, Madelyn Anderson, and Roger sat in Spencer's office, waiting for him to return from the washroom.

"Sorry about the wait," Spencer said on his return, "My Danish wanted to be on the outside today. He dabbed a paper towel over the wet spot on the front of his shirt. "Now, let's get to business. Roger has no doubt

filled you in, Madelyn, so let's brainstorm. I'm ready to consider anything."

"As of now, we spend fifty percent of our sales budget on print ads in magazines, ten percent in newspapers, and thirty-five percent online, which includes the website and ads on Facebook and other social media outlets. This leaves about five percent for promotions, billboards, and foreign outreach."

"Do we have any data on the cost/benefit of those percentages?"

Roger raised a finger and began, "Your father asked the same question, and I have been gathering information for a couple of months. It is incomplete, so I'm not sure of its accuracy, but from what I surmise so far, online ads that link to our website result in many sales, and that is trending upward. I think expanding our web presence would be a benefit."

"Perhaps online promotions with small discounts would work," added Madelyn.

"Let's give that a try and follow the results. I'm more curious about the money spent on magazine ads. Do we really get fifty percent of our sales from print ads?"

"Now that we've added QR codes to our print ads, people order online, so it's hard to say. The print ad leads them to us." Madelyn pulled her hair behind one ear and continued. "We thought about adding a survey question to the online order form. How did you hear about us? With multiple options to choose from. That would be a quick response from the customer but would help us focus our advertising budget."

"Great idea, Madelyn. Is that something our IT can do, or do we hire it out?"

"We pay a web designer already to keep our site up to date. I'll put the question together and let them know."

Roger cleared his throat. "These ideas will head us in the right direction, but are they enough? I feel like we need to do something big. Yeah, we've been around awhile, and yes, people have heard of us, but what can we do to get people to buy our products instead of the competition's?"

"Let's think on it," said Spencer, standing up. "Let's plan to meet Friday morning with ideas. In the meantime, focus on looking at new ways to communicate with the public."

Madelyn and Roger stood to leave.

Spencer opened his office door. "Thank you, Madelyn. Roger, could you stay for a minute."

"Sure."

After Madelyn left, Spencer closed the door. "You had said my father would sometimes visit the employees' break rooms and chat with them. Do you think if I did that it would be awkward at this point?"

"I think it might reassure them that the company is in good hands. There is a rumor that you are going to make big changes and maybe they'll be out of a job."

"What? Where did that come from?"

"People fear change. You are a change. They were used to your father's way, and they know from your division that you are not your father."

"You mean, I'm not as nice?"

"Well, you have the reputation of being . . . a bit sterner."

"Are you trying to say they think I'm a bull-headed stickler for details?"

"Let's say not as easy-going as your dad."

"You are quite the diplomat, Roger. But I get your meaning. Thank you."

Spencer opened the door and Roger made his exit.

***

At lunch the following day, Spencer made his way over to the Camping Supply building. He thought it best to start with Ronan's division, at least his brother would have his back should things get awkward. On his way, he walked past the landscaped lawns and flower beds. Red-leafed coleus and periwinkles blanketed the gardens along the buildings with clusters of hydrangeas and dahlias adding splashes of color. The smell of fresh-cut grass always reminded him of his childhood, playing tag or kickball in the backyard, or playing catch with his dad. A twinge of regret passed through his mind that he'd been busy with work and rarely had time for playing catch with Jay, and now Jay was grown and working.

Ronan met Spencer at the door and led him to the breakroom. The conversations stopped as they entered.

"Hi, everyone," Spencer began, "I thought I would continue my father's tradition of visiting with each division on occasion. We're in this together and hearing your successes and concerns will help CampWild be a stronger company."

No one spoke up. The employees looked at each other. Spencer could sense their unease, but he wasn't sure how to dissipate it. *Dad was so much more a people person than I am*, he thought.

Finally, an older man with thinning gray hair and thick glasses spoke. "Sorry for your loss, Mr. Ward. I know your grief is much greater than ours, but we miss your father also."

"Thank you. My father always said this company was his extended family, so I can understand your feelings. It was his wish to keep the company going. If there is anything I can do, please, let Ronan know. He will make sure I am made aware."

"Mr. Ward?" a young woman in a wheelchair began. "Your father was so kind. I want you to know that. When I was having trouble getting a job, you know, because," she indicated her wheelchair, "he insisted on hiring me and making my workstation wheelchair accessible. I am so grateful that I can be employed and productive."

Spencer was once again amazed at his father's care for others.

The ice seemed to be broken and the lunchroom conversations returned. Spencer chatted with a few employees and got to know a little about their backgrounds and interests. He realized he didn't even know this much about the employees in his former division even though some had worked there for years. *How could I be so clueless?* he thought. He made his exit and promised himself to make this a regular occurrence. Tomorrow, he'd visit his former division.

***

Spencer, Roger, and Madelyn reconvened Friday morning as scheduled.

"Before you share any ideas," Spencer began, "I want to tell you a story. Last night, my son was flipping through TV channels. He stopped at an advertisement for drones, the kind with the little camera that are not much more than remote-controlled cars that can fly. We watched for several minutes. It was quite interesting. And believe it or not, we ended up buying one. I had not even thought of it before that commercial, but it got me hooked. That's what we need to have, one of those long commercials that convince people they need our products."

"Infomercials," Roger said. "They are expensive."

"What are we talking about, a few thousand?"

"Mr. Ward, we had looked into doing an infomercial a couple of years ago but decided against it. It seemed too big of a risk when things were going well for the company. I can look up the figures, give me a second." Madelyn typed on her laptop and located the file. "Production would run about $300,000, and buying airtime will add to that considerably."

"What are you thinking, Spencer?" asked Roger.

Spencer rubbed his forehead. "That is a lot of money. But I think you are right, Roger, we have to do something big if we want to get this company back on solid footing. Let's crunch some numbers and see what we can come up with to finance this. We can pull some from the sales budget. Madelyn, look over the print budget and see if you can cut that down to forty percent. And get up-to-date quotes on production costs for an infomercial. I'll talk to the bank."

He stood up, indicating the meeting was over, then sat down again. "My apologies. I didn't even listen to your ideas."

Roger, already standing, shrugged his shoulders. "I was just going to suggest readjusting our expenditures to put more into online sales. There are many new opportunities for ad placements online."

"We should do that, too."

"And I thought we might target one or two big items to draw people to our website. Then they could see what else we have. Add-ons always increase sales if we can get the customer to buy something to start with," said Madelyn.

"Think on that one. See what the competition is doing."

Roger and Madelyn exited the office.

Spencer put his feet up on the desk and leaned back in his chair. He took long, slow, deep breaths, enjoying the moment of quiet. His first week as CEO had been a whirlwind of learning and decision making. There was a lot on his plate, but day by day, he told himself, he'd get through it and be a success.

He looked at the row of framed photos on his desk. He moved his father's photo to the center of the desk.

"Dad, I hope I can keep this place afloat. I'm trying my best," he said aloud. "Why didn't you tell me about the drop in sales? And why didn't you tell me about all of your anonymous gifts?"

Spencer didn't expect an answer from the photo, but he hoped asking out loud would help him understand. "Is it because I was always trying to increase profits? Trying to outdo the competition? Was I that focused on the money that I didn't see anything else?"

Recalling what his father said not long ago, "Helping people makes me happy," Spencer began putting the pieces together. His father had been telling him all along.

Am I happy? thought Spencer. He was not sure he liked the answer.

CHAPTER 6

Camping

"Are you sure?" Spencer asked for the fifth time in as many days. "This isn't too much for you, Ms. Hanson?"

"Mr. Ward, I'm quite confident I can handle this," Jen Hanson assured him. "My degree is in television and film production."

"Yes, your mother told me when I was having lunch with some of the tenting crew. That's why I had my assistant reach out to you. I know it's your first post-graduation production, and I'd like to help jump-start your career. But you can understand my concern."

"Of course."

Spencer noted at their first meeting, how mature she sounded in comparison to her looks. Even though she was twenty-two and a college graduate, she could almost pass for his daughter's age, and he couldn't picture giving so much responsibility to his daughter. He knew he shouldn't judge her abilities by her petite frame and youthful appearance.

Jen adjusted her ponytail and sat straight with an iPad in her lap, ready to work out the details of filming.

"Your idea of filming the employees using Camp-Wild products is great. It will save us from having to hire actors. I have an idea we invite their families for a

camping weekend and set up a full campsite. It would make a great background. You would, of course, have a say in who gets filmed for the infomercial. I have no idea what works visually for getting customers' attention and I understand you have also studied Marketing."

"It was part of my degree electives. With proper planning, we could get all of the featured products filmed in a short time. Did you have a date in mind?"

Spencer looked at his August calendar. "Last weekend this month. It gives us a little over two weeks to put it together. We'll use the wooded acreage at the back of the property. There is an open field for tenting. My dad used to take us camping back there as kids."

Jen raised her eyebrows. "Do you have any photos of those trips? We could use them to give a little company history and show that CampWild has been around for a while. Longevity means trustworthiness in the consumers' eyes."

"I think there might even be some Super 8 film of our camping trips. I'll have to ask my mother."

"Super 8, that's going back. Anything we find that might be useful for the production, I could get it digitized through the college."

"Isn't technology great? I should probably have all of the films digitized at some point."

Jen asked, "Would it be possible to look over the camping area? It would give me a better sense for planning purposes."

"Sure, we could go out now if you like."

Jen nodded.

Spencer pressed his intercom. "I'll be out of the office for an hour or so." He stood and ushered Jen to the door. "Beautiful day for a stroll."

In the hallway, they ran into Ronan.

"I was just stopping by to see you," Ronan said to Spencer. He turned and nodded to Jen, "Ms. Hanson."

"Join us," Spencer said, motioning. "We're on our way to Dad's old camping spot. We're planning to film the infomercial there during an employee camping weekend. We can talk on the way."

Ronan matched his pace with theirs. "It can wait. Home stuff. I haven't been out to the old camping spot in years. You never took the kids there?"

Spencer knew it wasn't a jab, but he felt a twinge of regret at his time management choices when it came to family. "I always seemed to be busy with other things."

"We won't mention any of that in the infomercial," Jen said. "Let's highlight the fun."

"And the quality of our products," Spencer added.

"I have an idea," Ronan offered. "Have someone trying to set up a competitor's tent, has trouble, and says, CampWild tents are so much easier to set up. Something like that."

"I like it," Spencer said, squeezing his younger brother's shoulder. He turned to Jen. "I know I repeat myself, but I think it is so important to stress the quality

of our products over the competitors' cheaper, but inferior gear. We have to give them a reason to spend more."

"Our products last longer, for sure," Ronan added. "And they can be trusted to work as advertised. That would be a good point, especially for the climbing equipment. No one wants a carabiner or a piton to fail halfway up a cliff face."

"We'll work that in," Jen added.

When they arrived, the first thing Spencer noticed was the field he remembered was partially overgrown. "We'll get the landscapers to clear this out and mow the weeds." He looked at the grove of oak trees on the east side of the field and the maples, birch, and aspen to the north and west.

"That shagbark hickory is still here," Ronan pointed out. "Remember when we used to throw the nuts at each other?"

"I remember getting into trouble even though you started it," Spencer reminded him."

"The price you pay for being the older brother."

"I'll tell you a secret, little brother, I never minded when my punishment was to gather wood. I liked to do that. I got to explore the woods on my own."

"Dad thought you were off sulking."

"Well, maybe in the beginning. Now, back to business." Spencer held his arms wide. "What do you think of the place, Ms. Hanson?"

She walked around some more, looking up and

facing different directions. "We'll need to be particular about where tents get set up so we can take advantage of the natural lighting, but yes, this is great. Can we get a SUV up here with the equipment?"

"Sure," answered Spencer.

"Great. My assistant will be so happy he doesn't have to slog it all from the parking lot."

The three started back down the sloping hill toward the parking lot behind the newest CampWild building. Spencer felt something small bounce off his back. He turned. Ronan, standing a few feet behind with his arm raised, started laughing, another hickory nut in his hand.

"I'm not even tempted, Ronan," Spencer said.

"You're no fun."

Jen laughed. "Brotherly love, I guess."

***

The weekend of the campout and video shoot arrived with warm, sunny weather. Fourteen families decided to participate, a total of fifty-eight people, including Spencer, Jay, and Rachel. Spencer's wife was busy with her ladies' group fundraiser for the weekend, but Spencer looked on the bright side. *I get to spend some quality time with my kids before they are completely grown.*

All participating employees were allowed to leave work at noon to start the campout. Jen wanted the afternoon sun for the shots of setting up the tents and campsites.

"Each family gets a tent. They are marked by size, so look for the name when you distribute them," Spencer instructed two employees who brought the supplies up in one of the company's delivery trucks.

"Do we give out the grills and lanterns and the rest at the same time?"

"If I may interrupt," said Jen, "could we get shots of the tents being set up first? I don't want to be tripping over piles of supplies."

"No problem. We'll wait," said one of the men.

Jen and her cameraman scurried off to start filming. Her assistant tagged along with a clipboard for video releases and over his shoulder, a large, canvas bag of microphones, diffusers, and other equipment.

"Once all the camping equipment gets distributed, we'll make a run to get the food for dinner," Spencer said. "We'll bring up the food for each meal in time for it to be prepared. We'll use CampWild coolers. Jen will want shots of the food prep also."

A young girl and her father approached Spencer.

"Afternoon, Mr. Ward. This is such a treat. Thank you."

"No, thank *you*. Making this infomercial with real campers is going to be great."

"My daughter has a question for you. Go ahead, honey."

The little girl, who was no more than five years old,

looked Spencer in the eyes and asked, "When do we get the s'mores?"

"How about after dinner? When the sun goes down and we get the campfire started. Does that sound good?"

She nodded and buried her face into her father's leg.

"Thank you, Mr. Ward," the man said. He lifted his daughter onto his hip and walked away.

Spencer turned to the truck driver, "Totally forgot about s'mores. Could you run into town and pick up s'mores-making goodies?" He took out his wallet and handed the driver $200. "Enough for fifty-eight people."

Ronan, who caught the end of the conversation, said, "Dodged a bullet there, brother."

"Hey, I'm new at this. What's that they say, thank heaven for little girls? So true in this case. Speaking of girls, where is Beth?"

"She'll be here after work. I don't think she's keen on being on film."

Ronan and Spencer walked over to watch Jen interviewing campers as they set up their tents.

"Relax, don't be nervous," Jen urged. "Pretend you are chatting with a friend about your new tent. Let's start again."

It was clear the couple on camera were too nervous and it showed.

"Ronan," asked Spencer, "Isn't she from your division?"

"Yes. Kara."

Spencer waved a hand to get Jen's attention. "Perhaps if they chatted with Ronan. They know him."

The relieved look on Jen's face was all he needed. "I'll record an introduction of Ronan as head of the . . . "

"Camping Supplies division," finished Ronan.

"Then you can ask them questions."

Jen proceeded to film the interactions between Ronan, Kara, and her husband, stopping a couple of times to make sure Ronan covered the necessary talking points.

After a few minutes, Jen exclaimed, "Success." She and her assistant moved on to a family setting up a much larger tent while Spencer and Ronan walked among the other campers.

"You are a natural, Ronan. Maybe you missed your calling."

"I'm too much of a homebody to want to jet-set all over the world making movies."

"Understood. And what would I do without you here, heading up the most successful division?"

"There's that." The brothers laughed. Spencer felt something inside. It wasn't just the laugh of a good joke. It was a connection, a bond that he hadn't felt in a long while. *Why?* he wondered. Then it occurred to him. He had complimented his brother, and it had made his brother happy. And Spencer felt happy as well.

His father's words echoed through his thoughts again. *Making people happy makes me happy.*

Should we start distributing the cooking gear and picnic tables," Ronan asked, "now that the tents are mostly up?"

"If you would see to that, I'll set up a campfire ring and gather wood," Spencer replied.

"Old habits?"

"Memories."

As Ronan headed to the delivery truck, Spencer made his way into the woods under the oak trees, hoping to find some large branches to burn. He remembered his father telling him that oak burned slower than pine and popped less. *It wouldn't be good to scare the kids with loud, popping, hot pine sap.*

Fallen branches of all sizes were plentiful. No one had camped in the area for years. Spencer brought back armloads and piled them near the old fire ring. It took him only a few minutes to set the stones back in a circle.

Jay and a couple of other teen boys approached.

"Need any help, Dad?" asked Jay.

"If you boys want to gather up some more firewood, that would be great. I think there are a couple of folding saws in the truck. Ask your Uncle Ronan. He's there."

"Let's go," Jay said to the others, and off they went to the truck.

Spencer watched his son and the other two teens go. *I don't remember ever volunteering to help my father when I was their age. Was I that selfish?*

He returned to the woods for one last load. There was a peacefulness he felt there, away from all of the stresses of business and life. He stopped to look around and listen. A squirrel darted up a nearby tree. He could identify the chirps of the chickadees and nuthatches and the singsong of the titmouse, all things he learned from his parents in these very woods. In the distance, he could make out the tapping of a woodpecker.

He was startled from his reverie by the sounds of the boys, followed by Jen and her assistant.

"I thought we could get a shot of the boys using the camp saws."

"Great idea. Could I just have a minute? Boys, be silent and listen for the birds."

As they listened, Spencer identified the ones he could remember.

"I didn't know you knew all that, Dad," Jay said.

"I guess we should go camping some more. Anyway, let's not hold up our photographers."

The boys got to work, and Spencer took his load back to the campfire ring. He realized that there were things Jay did not know about him, just as there were things he did not know about his father.

He prepared the fire lay in the fire ring and brought over a few folding camp chairs and folding stools with Ronan's help.

"That's enough for now. We'll tell everyone to bring their chairs."

Jen continued filming as the families cooked their dinners on their new camp stoves with cookware and utensil kits provided by CampWild. The quick setup canopies and folding camp tables brought the whole scene to life.

Patty arrived in time to be filmed as Jay and Rachel were about to finish cooking dinner. Jen made a point of rounding up Spencer and Patty to be filmed with their kids.

"I'll interview with you on Monday in your office, Mr. Ward. This is just footage to show off the CampWild products being used by the owner's family. Pretend I'm not here."

After a few minutes, Jen and her crew moved on.

Spencer turned to his wife. "Thank you, Patty, for being a good sport."

"Are you staying, Mom?" Rachel asked.

"No. The ladies need me at the fundraiser. It's our big annual event. I'll see you at home tomorrow. Have fun." With that, she got up and made her way back down through the field to the parking lot.

***

As the sun was fading in the west, and before it was too late for the little kids to enjoy the campfire, Spencer broke out the s'mores ingredients and marshmallow roasting sticks. Jen was able to film an abundance of smiles and laughter.

One of the dads brought out a guitar and led everyone in lively renditions of "This Land is Your Land" and "On Top of Spaghetti," which he had to sing twice to the delight of several giggly preschoolers. They could hardly sit still until they got to the part where they could sneeze as loud as possible.

Spencer knew the guitar player from his former division but did not know until now that he played guitar. "Awesome entertainment, Sam," Spencer called out between songs. Sam played a few more sing-alongs and stopped when the kids started getting fussy.

"More tomorrow night," Sam responded when the kids wanted him to keep going.

The families made their way to the tents. Jen made sure to film the CampWild lanterns and flashlights.

"This was great, Mr. Ward," Jen said. "We'll be heading out for tonight. What time is breakfast? I want the viewers to smell the bacon and home fries."

"Cooked on CampWild camping cookware."

"Of course."

"I'm guessing about eight, so they'll be up by seven-thirtyish."

"We'll be here." She and her assistant, equipment in hand, made their way to her Jeep and drove off.

Spencer had a tent to himself. His kids insisted on setting up their tent. *Knowing teenagers, they'll probably be up half the night talking.*

He settled into his sleeping bag, his mind still racing. He couldn't help but imagine how the finished infomercial would look and if it would increase business for CampWild. But that wasn't all. There was so much happiness around the campfire, and Spencer felt it. Again, his father's words came to mind: *Making people happy makes me happy.*

***

After breakfast, Jay brought out his drone and flew it over the campsite, recording video and photos. He let the other teens give it a try. They were laughing at the photos and videos of each other when Jen approached the group.

"Jay, may I see?"

"Sure." Jay showed her a couple of the videos on his phone, which started the teens laughing again.

"I have a proposition for you. If you would fly the drone and get some images and videos for me, I'll give you production credits."

"Really?" Jay didn't need convincing. "I'll do it."

They spent the next hour filming the campsite at various angles with campers staged using CampWild products. Jen directed some campers to look up at the drone and wave.

She turned to Jay and said, "Not sure how much of this we will use. I hope no one gets upset if their big moment isn't in the final product."

"There's always the next one," Jay responded.

"You are quite the optimist, Jay. Thank you for your help. Here's my card if you could send them to that email."

"Sure thing."

Spencer and Ronan walked out of the woods and came over to Jen and Jay.

"Everything going okay?" Spencer asked.

"Your son, the master drone operator, got some outstanding images," Jen said.

Jay blushed. Ronan nudged Jay. "Maybe you could get a shot of your dad, outstanding in his field."

"That's a groan, Uncle Ronan. A dad joke and you're not even a dad."

"It doesn't hurt to practice," Ronan countered.

Jay held out the drone controller to Ronan and his father. "Do you want to try?"

Ronan was the first to take the controller. After careful instructions from Jay, he still managed to crash the drone into a nearby tent.

"Maybe you should be outstanding in a field," Spencer said to his brother.

"It's not as easy as it looks." Ronan handed the controller to Spencer.

Nothing ever is, thought Spencer. "Maybe we can get some shots of the CampWild buildings. Show people we're big and ready for their business."

***

The sunrise on Sunday morning filled the eastern sky with orange and yellow. The chickadees and nuthatches chattered away as the campers emerged from their tents. Spencer greeted the driver as he arrived with dozens of bagels and donuts, milk, cereals, and orange juice. Today was go-home day, and Jen would be arriving shortly to film. Spencer wanted the infomercial to include how easy and fast CampWild products were to pack up.

When most of the campers were out of their tents, Spencer called their attention.

"I want to thank you all for coming camping with us. It's been great fun, and you are all movie stars in my book."

The assembled group laughed and clapped. Someone shouted, "Thank you, Mr. Ward," to which more clapping ensued.

"But wait, there's more," Spencer said, mimicking an old advertising slogan. "And to show my appreciation, and so you can continue having fun, all of the CampWild products you've used this weekend, I would like you to keep them. And please take your families camping."

The sounds of hooting, hollering, and clapping rose again. Once it settled down, Spencer continued. "Here's Jen now. Let's get packing."

CHAPTER 7

Good Works

"I think you have nothing to worry about as far as the employees accepting you as the new CEO," said Roger. "They see a lot of your father in you. Although most of what he did was anonymous, there was certainly enough of his generosity showing."

Spencer shifted in his office chair. Somehow, he felt more at ease sitting there listening to the positive comparisons to his father. "I don't know how my father managed to be so generous to so many and still keep this company afloat."

"CampWild was more successful than he let on to most people. Everyone knew the company did well. We are the largest employer around here. But John didn't like the idea of people asking him for money for this or that. He liked the anonymous angel mystique. He didn't want the accolades."

"Or criticism for that matter," added Steve.

"Criticism?" asked Spencer.

"Oh, you know. A person gives to a certain cause and gets negative press because they should have donated to a different, more worthy, cause."

"Good grief. Now I understand the anonymous part. But the company isn't doing as well now and hasn't been for a couple of years."

Steve sat up in his chair. "To be honest, I think your father cared less about big profits in the end. He wanted to make sure he did things for people that mattered, things that would make a difference in their lives."

"He never told us he had cancer," added Roger, "but we could sense a shift in his focus. Never could figure it out, though."

Steve shrugged. "I just wrote it off as his being confident in the company's ongoing success, not having to worry about finances."

"But certainly, he knew sales were slowing?" Spencer asked.

"Oh, sure, but the company has had its ups and downs over the years," Roger pointed out.

"Let's hope this infomercial keeps us from going down and out." Spencer had less confidence in the company's future now that the weight of that future rested on his shoulders.

Spencer's intercom buzzed.

"Martin is here for your ten o'clock."

Roger and Steve stood to leave.

"Please stay. I could use your input. Human resources and I haven't always seen eye to eye on hiring."

Roger and Steve sat back down. Martin entered with a folder of papers and set them on the conference table.

"Morning, everyone," Martin said, maintaining a dry business tone. "These are all of the applications we've received for the open position in your old division,

Tenting. They need a machine operator on the three-to-eleven shift. We need to narrow this to three candidates for Jina to interview."

Martin opened the folder and skimmed each, giving the men a brief overview of each candidate's work history and background. Spencer was finding it difficult to rule out any.

Martin skimmed another and let "Oh," slip out as he tossed the application into the trash.

Curious, Spencer asked," Why did you do that?"

"Ex-con."

Roger retrieved the application from the trash and handed it to Spencer, who looked it over.

"This man is an Eagle Scout and a volunteer fire-fighter. I think we should have him in for an interview," Spencer said. "Give him a chance to explain."

"But he's an ex-con," Martin implored. "You're asking for trouble."

"I didn't say we'd hire him, but I think I'd like to have him in. People make mistakes. It says he served a year in minimum security, so it was not a violent crime. What's the harm?"

Martin took a moment before responding. "I was hoping with you now at the helm, hiring would be less complicated. Your father had a soft spot for those kinds of people."

Roger spoke up. "I guess it runs in the family, but I can't think of any hire John approved that ended badly."

"Set up an interview as soon as possible and have Jina here as well," Spencer instructed.

Martin took the folder from the table and started toward the door.

"Keep those applications handy, though," Spencer added.

After Martin left the office, Steve said, "You surprise me, Spencer. I didn't think you'd take that kind of risk."

"Part of me wanted to leave that application in the trash, but another part wants to see if I can help."

"You are more like your father than you know," Steve said.

***

Jina entered Spencer's office and walked over to the window. "Nice view."

Spencer laughed, knowing it was almost the same view from his old office, now Jina's office.

"I see you still have your sense of humor. Tenting is still going well?"

"Yes. I'm curious. Why the change in hiring interviews though?"

"Not a permanent change. This interview is a little different." Spencer explained the circumstances.

"I see."

Spencer called for the candidate to come in.

A thin, medium-height young man entered. His hair looked recently cut. The suit jacket he wore looked worn and slightly large for his frame. It was obvious to Spencer that the young man was trying his hardest to make a good impression.

"Robert Murphy, correct?" Spencer asked.

Robert nodded. "Yes. Thank you for interviewing me, Mr. Ward."

"This is Jina Smith, head of the Tenting division."

"Nice to meet you, Ms. Smith."

"Have a seat, "Spencer pointed to a chair at the conference table opposite himself and Jina.

Once seated, Robert looked around the office. "This is very nice."

"Thank you, Robert." Spencer wondered if Robert had been to interview training. Complimenting a future employer's office is a way to get on their good side. "I've read your application, so tell us about yourself and why you want to work for CampWild."

"You know I was in prison. I know I need to address that right away. I did something stupid. I fudged the books at my previous employer and took some money I shouldn't have. If you want to end the interview now, I'll understand."

"I already knew about your incarceration from your application, and here we are. I like a man willing to admit his mistakes. Now, the job opening we have is for a machine operator in the Tenting division. No handling money or finances in any form. We won't need to worry about that."

Spencer watched as the young man's shoulders relaxed. "The job is second shift, three to eleven."

"I'll take any time. I need a job. I have a five-year-old son and we've been living off my wife's waitressing money and loans from her parents."

Jina asked, "So, you are home with your son while your wife works?"

"Now, yes, when I'm not looking for work. He spent a lot of time with babysitters when I was in prison, so it's been good catching up. If he needs to continue with a sitter, we'll manage. Luckily, he's started school, so he's there during the day. I want to be a good dad and husband. I have to make up for not being there for so long."

"We have a policy here at CampWild that if a position opens in a different shift or area, employees are given the first choice over new hires," Jina explained. "If you were to work here, there would be a possibility of changing shifts so you could be home in the evenings with your son."

"Everyone says this is a great place to work. I can see why." Robert blushed. "I didn't mean that to sound . . ."

"It was from the heart," said Jina. "Compliment accepted."

Spencer stood up. "Jina will take you on a tour of the Tenting division and show you the job specifics. Then we'll make our decision and let you know."

"Thank you, Mr. Ward. It was nice to meet you."

Jina ushered Robert out of the office.

Spencer sat in his high-back office chair and closed his eyes. He and the young man were similar. Both wanted to provide for their families. Spencer was impressed by Robert's willingness to express his feelings about being a good father. Again, a pang of guilt that he didn't remember having the same level of concern about his children, or at least not being able to express it openly. When they were little, Patty was a stay-at-home mom, and he focused on his job at CampWild. *There's something to be said for wanting to be a good dad.*

Spencer realized he had already made up his mind to hire the guy.

***

"Robert will be a good fit, I think," Jina informed Spencer when she stopped by that afternoon.

"Great, let's hire him asap."

"We may have another opening in the Tenting division soon. Are there more candidates for me to interview?"

"Another opening?"

"Margery Davis may be leaving."

"Good ol' Marge. But she's close to retirement. Why would she leave?"

"Her husband, Harvey, has Type 1 diabetes and has been having serious heart issues for the last year or

more. Lately, it's become much worse. He's about to go into hospice care. If he does, she wants to be with him."

"Understandable, but it doesn't sound like an if, it sounds like a definite."

"I'm afraid so."

"Tell Marge she doesn't have to quit. We'll give her leave starting tomorrow. She should be with him like my mother was for my dad. No one should be alone at a time like this. And tell her we'll keep her pay coming as if she were here. I don't want her to worry about that."

"And her position?"

"We can hire someone as a temp, with the possibility of making it permanent if something opens up. I'll send over a couple of possibilities after I see Martin in HR."

"She will be so relieved. Thank you."

"It's the right thing to do." Spencer walked Jina to his office door and closed it behind her.

Spencer felt a wave of panic. *What is happening to me?* Spencer went from feeling great about his generosity towards Marge to anxiety over the company's financial situation. He tried to convince himself that the company's fortunes had risen and fallen several times in the past and that this latest situation was no different. *That infomercial has to work.*

***

The following week, Jen brought the rough cut of the infomercial for Spencer to preview. He called Roger and Steve in, as well as the division heads, to get their feedback.

"At this point, I'll insert the Super 8 footage of your dad and your family once I get the digital conversions back," Jen said when the screen went black. "And we'll add your comments about the fun you had camping as a kid."

After the presentation, she listened to their comments and took notes.

"It looks great," Spencer said, attempting to wrap up the discussion.

"I agree," said Steve. "And I have been staying up late watching lots of infomercials to get a feel for them. This will stand out. It has more action and real-life demonstrations of our products."

"Now, we just have to hope it translates into sales," commented Roger.

Ronan spoke up. "Will we get to see the Super 8 parts before it gets broadcast? I want to know if I should warn my fiancée about my scrawny boy phase."

With that, everyone laughed.

Steve and Roger stayed back as the others left.

"Did you read about Deihl's Dairy and Donuts?" Roger asked Spencer.

"The ice cream shop in town? No, what about them?"

"The paper said they are going to have to give up sponsorship of the kid's baseball team, but so far no one has stepped up to take over."

"Do you want CampWild to be the new sponsor?"

"We thought we'd bring it up," said Steve.

Spencer was trying to calculate how much he'd already committed to Marge and the infomercial. "We need to recoup our infomercial expenses before I can commit. I don't want to say yes and then have to rescind it in a year or two. Deihl's has been the team sponsor for as long as I can remember, even back when I played."

Roger and Steve sat quietly.

"Okay, I'll ask. What would my father have done?"

"I know he didn't like being asked to give money. If we sponsored the team, it might end up in a never-ending parade of teams wanting sponsorships. Then, where do we draw the line without offending one sport or another?"

"I have an idea," Spencer said. "My dad liked to be anonymous. What if we anonymously donate enough money for Deihl's to keep their sponsorship? Everybody wins."

"You are starting to think like your dad," Steve said.

"And I think I'm starting to feel like he did, happy to be making others happy. So, who wants to make the drop-off?"

Both Steve and Roger raised their hands, but Roger gave in to Steve.

"I'll get my suit from the closet," Steve said, getting up. "I'll get the no-name money orders and drop them off at Deihl's with a note explaining the donation."

"You're sure they won't know," asked Spencer.

"We're pros at this," Steve assured him. "Like ninjas." He did chops with his arms and the three men laughed.

After the two assistants left the office, Spencer stood at the window. Looking out at the buildings and full parking lots, it was clear to him how important Camp-Wild was to the financial health of the community. He felt that weight more than ever now that the future of CampWild was in his hands.

How did Dad do this and not feel overwhelmed?

Spencer never considered himself to be good at introspection, but lately, it seemed necessary. His father started the business and oversaw its growth one step at a time. Spencer convinced himself that is why his father didn't feel the pressure; he had grown with the company. Spencer was walking into a position that was already large and well established.

For now, Spencer satisfied his brain with that thought, and it gave him some sense of relief that he would manage. *I'm a quick learner,* he assured himself.

***

Spencer woke early, and in the quiet dimness of the room, realized he had been dreaming about Marge and her ailing husband. He saw her crying at her husband's bedside while monitors beeped and whirred, and nurses came and went. He felt the urge to help.

Spencer was dressed and was eating his breakfast by the time his wife woke.

"You are up early," she noted as she walked into the kitchen.

"I thought I'd stop into the hospice center and check on Marge and her husband on my way to the office."

"Sometimes you surprise me," Patty said. When Spencer gave her a puzzled look, she added, "In a good way." She ran her fingers through her hair, straightening the tangles.

Spencer wasn't sure how to process Patty's statement. *Was it a criticism or a compliment? Probably both,* he mused, *but not worth pursuing now.* Instead, he focused on his mission. "Marge has worked for CampWild for many years. It seems like the right thing to do."

"I agree. Maybe pick up some flowers on your way."

"Good idea," Spencer said, taking another piece of toast with him as he headed out the door. He wanted to stop and kiss Patty as he passed her, but they had stopped that tradition a long time ago.

***

Spencer arrived at the hospice center with a colorful bouquet. The florist suggested a selection that was mildly scented to avoid the hospice center not allowing it.

He took a deep breath and walked toward the entrance. He wrestled with his nervousness, trying to convince himself not to turn back. *It seemed like a good idea this morning, but now that I'm here, it's very stressful.* Spencer knew his relationship with employees was distant, even with long-time employees like Marge. He had to admit that he knew very little about her other than she was a dependable worker. *Will Marge think I'm intruding?* He shook that thought from his mind. Another deep breath. *I'm here. I can do this.*

Despite his apprehensions, he opened the door.

A young smiling receptionist directed him down the hall to room twenty-seven. Her pleasant disposition seemed both necessary and out of place considering what the hospice center's purpose was.

He peered into the open doorway. Marge looked up from her seat by the bed. Her eyes widened and she placed a hand on her chest. She stood, wiping the corners of her eyes with a folded white handkerchief. She patted the creases on her clothing and approached Spencer, holding a finger to her lips.

"He's sleeping now," Marge whispered.

They stepped into the hallway.

"What a surprise to see you, Mr. Ward. It's so kind of you. And what lovely flowers," Marge said, taking the bouquet of multicolored mums and white daisies.

"The florist calls it Ray of Sunshine. I thought it would cheer him up."

"It has cheered me up already. It is so thoughtful of you to stop by."

"I wanted to show my support. Did you spend the whole night here?"

"Yes. The staff is quite nice about everything. They gave me a cot to rest on. I'm thankful to not be alone during this. I wouldn't be able to keep track of all of his needs like these nurses do."

"You're never alone, Marge. Your CampWild family will be here for you." Spencer heard himself saying those things, but part of his mind was thinking *Where did that come from?* The idea that CampWild was like a family was not how he thought of his employees. Until now.

"That is comforting to know," Marge said, "I am grateful you are giving me this time to be with Harvey." Her eyes began to well.

Coughing and rustling of blankets from within the room interrupted their conversation. Marge dabbed her eyes and pulled Spencer into the room.

"Good morning, dear. Look who brought us some cheerful flowers. Spencer Ward. From CampWild."

Harvey tried to sit up. Marge stuffed pillows behind him. His short gray hair was standing on end.

"If I had known we were having company, I would have shaved," Harvey joked.

"Not a problem," said Spencer. "I see that same look every morning in the mirror." Spencer could see that Harvey was having trouble catching his breath even with the oxygen tube under his nose. "I was just stopping by on my way to work to say hello."

"Very kind of you, Mr. Ward. Marge has always said nice things about you." Harvey paused, then winked. "I try not to get jealous."

"Oh, stop," Marge said, laughing and giving Harvey's arm a squeeze.

"It's nice to see you in good spirits, Harvey. I've got to run."

"Thank you again," Marge said as she walked Spencer to the door.

Spencer was glad the visit went well, and that Harvey seemed to be in good spirits. Stepping out of his comfort zone to bring a little happiness to Marge and her husband made him feel better. *Dad was right. Making people happy makes me happy.* His thoughts drifted to his father's death and funeral. Many people had shared their stories about his father, most all about how his father had brought them happiness in one way or another.

As he started his car, he forced himself to return his thoughts to the present. CampWild needed his full attention if it was going to succeed.

CHAPTER 8
Trouble

"**Y**our wife is on line three."

Spencer picked up the receiver and pushed the button. "What's up?"

"I hope you can free up an hour or so. I just got a call from the school. Jay is about to be suspended for a week."

"You're kidding. Why?"

"Something about a fight. The vice-principal didn't give details. Said he wanted a parent to meet with him as soon as possible."

"Jay? In a fight? That's so unlike him."

"Will you go down?"

Spencer sighed. "Give me a few minutes to wrap up here. I'll go straight there." He hung up the phone and tagged his current work with a sticky note, placing it in his top drawer.

While he prepared to leave, he thought about Jay. They hadn't spoken much beyond short casual conversations lately. Spencer had a pang of guilt. *Maybe I don't know Jay as well as I should. Maybe I should spend more time with him. But then again, he's sixteen and wants his space.* Somehow, that thought didn't make Spencer feel better.

***

"Mr. Ward. To see the vice-principal," Spencer said without emotion while standing at the school's entrance, looking into the security camera. *It would be good to learn the man's name*, thought Spencer.

The door buzzed and he entered the lobby and approached the secretary.

"Sign here," she said, pointing to a clipboard on the counter.

While the secretary notified the vice-principal, Spencer looked around. The lobby hadn't changed much since he went there, except for new paint, a mural celebrating diversity, and security cameras in several locations to cover the area from every angle.

"Have a seat, Mr. Ward. The vice-principal will call for you shortly."

Spencer sat on the bench beneath the mural. Several high school students walked by, laughing and joking around. *Boy, do I feel old.*

One of the students looked over his shoulder at Spencer, giving him a puzzled look. *Why do I feel guilty sitting here?* thought Spencer. Then he remembered. *I'll bet this is the same bench kids sit at when they are in trouble. Some things never change.*

Several minutes later, the vice-principal stepped out of his office and walked toward Spencer.

"Mr. Ward. Nice to meet you. Please, step into my office."

Spencer did as he was asked and had a seat. He expected Jay to be in the room, but he and the vice-principal were alone.

"Where is Jay?" Spencer asked.

"Jay? Oh, John."

"He goes by Jay. He's named after his grandfather, John Ward."

"John will be joining us shortly, but I wanted to speak with you regarding the incident first."

Spencer wondered if he was being primed to take the vice-principal's side before Jay had a chance to explain his actions, but he kept that thought to himself.

"This morning at lunch, Jay and another student got into a fight in the cafeteria. Punches were thrown by both boys. The school's zero-tolerance policy for fighting means each will receive one week of out-of-school suspension."

"I'm not following. Why am I here if this is already decided? Don't we get to hear the circumstances? What caused it? Who started it?"

"Our district's zero-tolerance policy makes who started it irrelevant. I've spoken to John. He understands the consequences of his actions. You are here to take John home."

"One question. How does your policy affect college applications, scholarships, that kind of thing?"

"That is a question for the school board, I'm afraid."

There was a knock on the door.

"Come in," called the vice-principal.

Jay opened the door and looked at his father. Spencer could see Jay blinking back tears. He quickly stood and walked Jay out of the building without another word to the vice-principal.

Once in the car, Jay let the tears fall. "I'm sorry, Dad."

"First, tell me what happened."

Jay cleared his throat. I know you'll believe what they told you, but it's not what happened."

"Let me decide after you tell me." Spencer was surprised that Jay would assume he wouldn't believe him. *My son doesn't trust me to be on his side.*

"This kid was eating his lunch alone like he always does, and these jerks were throwing little bits of food at his head and onto his lunch tray and laughing. My friends and I could see he was getting upset. He has Asperger's or something. So, I said 'knock it off.'" Jay paused.

"Okay. That sounds appropriate. Then?"

"Then one of those kids told me to mind my own business. I told him what he was doing was my business. He came over and pushed my head into the table." Jay lifted the front of his hair and Spencer could see the red skin on his forehead.

"Ouch. Then what?"

"When I stood up, he punched me in the chest, and I fell back onto the table. I tried to block his punches." Jay demonstrated holding his arms up while he spoke.

"He is a lot bigger than I am. Luckily, the Resource Office showed up. The kid claimed I started it and he was defending himself. His friends said the same thing. My friends were scared to get involved after seeing what happened to me."

"The Resource Officer told the vice-principal I was punching too."

"Did you tell the vice-principal what you told me?"

"He wouldn't listen. He kept saying 'zero tolerance for fighting.'"

"I got the same message. In your defense, you were not wrong to defend that boy."

"I'm suspended, though."

"Let's not get into the politics of that. I'm glad you said something. No one should have to put up with bullies."

"I should have said something the first day they bothered him. Maybe it wouldn't have escalated to this."

"Don't second guess yourself. You did what you thought was right. I'm proud of you, Jay. There is nothing ever wrong with being kind."

Spencer glanced over toward Jay. He watched Jay's shoulders settle and the tenseness on his face diminish.

Jay smiled. "Grandpa always said it doesn't hurt to be kind."

"That he did."

"But I don't think he was thinking about anyone fighting afterward."

Spencer laughed. "No, I don't imagine he did. How about you come to work with me for the rest of the day?"

"Sure."

When Spencer pulled into the parking lot, he spotted Jen's Jeep.

"It looks like the infomercial is ready," Spencer said.

"Am I in it?" asked Jay.

"We'll find out shortly."

They hurried into the building and up to Spencer's office.

"Sorry to keep you waiting, Jen. Had to pick up Jay at school."

"No problem. Whenever you're ready."

Spencer assembled his team to watch the ad together. "Think like a customer. Would you buy our products?"

Roger dimmed the office lights, and everyone sat in silence while the infomercial played.

"Well?" started Spencer as Roger turned up the lights, "I'd like to hear everyone's first reaction. Yes or No."

There was a chorus of Yes.

"Any questions or concerns?" Spencer asked.

"No, but I think Jen did a good job presenting the diversity of people who could use our products," Steve said.

"It helps that we have a very diverse workforce," Spencer replied. "Jay, I'm going to put you on the spot since you represent young people here. What did you think?"

Jay looked around the room. "There were a lot of young people on the camping trip, and this showed them–us–having fun. Maybe this will get kids to get away from their video games for a while and go camping."

"Good point." Spencer turned to Jen. "So, how soon can we go on air?"

"I have lined up spots starting Friday night, so I'll make them official now that I have your approval."

"Let's do it."

***

Late that afternoon, Jay was sitting at the table in Spencer's office, playing on his phone, when Steve popped in.

"Sorry to bother you, but I just got off the phone with CCHB."

"About?"

"Your father was trying to strike a deal with them to offer our product line at their stores. There were some differences of opinion about the wholesale prices, so the deal fell through. Now, they are willing to start up discussions again. I think this is a good sign for us, a good bargaining position to be in."

"Let's set up a meeting," Spencer said. "I'm open."

Jay spoke. "I know CCHB sells camping stuff, but what does CCHB stand for?

"Camping, Climbing, Hiking, Boating," Steve answered. "They're a big national chain. We could do well by them if the terms are good."

"Let's hope," Spencer said.

***

As weeks passed, the volume of orders continued to climb. Spencer met with his two assistants to go over the figures.

"That infomercial did the trick," exclaimed Roger. "We're going to have to increase production. The stock in our warehouse is emptying faster than we can replace it. And we're about to enter the holiday buying season."

"True, and the CCHB deal is a factor also," Spencer explained. "They were willing to meet our offer after so many people came to their stores asking about Camp-Wild products. They had heard about us through the infomercial."

"Their profit helps our profit," Roger said.

"Exactly," replied Spencer.

"Speaking of increasing production, we eliminated a third shift years ago. Do we bring it back?" asked Steve.

Spencer studied the sales figures on his computer screen. "Most of the sales are in tenting and camping supplies. Let's start with a three-day-a-week, eleven-to-three shift in those divisions. We'll get Martin to get job opening notices out. Let's make them temp positions until we know for sure the upswing is steady."

CHAPTER 9

The Unexpected

On the quiet drive to his office, Spencer was sensing something was different in his life. He wasn't sure what, but it felt good. *Maybe,* he thought, *it's because the company is doing well.* He couldn't be sure. The company had done well before.

The heavy rain didn't sour his good mood as he made his way into CampWild's main building.

"Morning, Gracie," he said as he passed her desk.

"Morning, Mr., Ward."

He sat at the conference table in his office with his computer and various printouts in front of him. He realized he was being too conservative on his growth projections. Over the last three months, orders doubled on some items and tripled on others, and it took running a third shift five days a week and adding Saturday production to keep up with demand. The usual January to February, post-holiday dip in sales allowed their warehouse to restock in anticipation of the upcoming spring surge in sales, but that was looking to be a record season.

Roger stepped into the office and sat for their morning meeting.

"It's hard to believe I was worried we'd go under," Spencer confided.

"Things have a way of working out," Roger offered, leaning back in his chair at the conference table.

"You sound like my father," Spencer said.

"It's what your father used to say."

"If it weren't for the workers, we'd be nowhere."

"Your father used to say that, too."

Spencer smiled. "Granted, we made the infomercial, but the workers made the products. It feels like a team effort." Spencer paused. "I'm sounding more like a coach than a boss, but that's what I'm feeling."

Roger nodded. "Your father said CampWild was his extended family."

Spencer immediately recalled his conversation with Marge. *You're CampWild family,* he had said. A sudden warm feeling passed through him. "Roger, I think Dad was right. We are like a family."

"Can I call you Pops then?"

"Wait a minute, you are older than I am."

The two were laughing when Steve entered the office.

"What did I miss?"

"A family meeting," said Roger. "I think that makes you the weird cousin."

Steve looked at them both. "I have no idea what you two are talking about. I'm not sure I want to know."

Spencer explained, "We were just thinking how CampWild is like an extended family."

It was clear to Spencer how his relationship with

Roger and Steve had developed in the past few months. He considered them friends now. In some ways, a secret fraternity of anonymous gift-givers distributing help to those in need.

"I know we give a holiday bonus every year, but this year feels different," continued Spencer. "We're more than solvent. We're rolling in dough, as they say. It feels right to share some of that with the employees. Don't you think?"

"No argument from me," Roger said.

"Me either," added Steve.

"I'm thinking something big. What if we took one million of these profits and distributed it among the employees? All of them."

"Wow," said Steve, wide-eyed. "Are you sure?"

"We've netted over ten million in six months. I'm sure."

Steve shook his head. "Your CFO is going to freak out, poor guy. He is so careful with every dime."

"Yes, that's why we're in such good shape. So now is the time to celebrate." Spencer let a wide grin spread across his face.

Roger and Steve sat staring.

"I haven't lost my mind. We can do this."

Steve exhaled. "Okay. Detail question: Does every-one get the same amount?"

Spencer thought for a moment. "Let's base it on how long they've worked here and what position they have.

But no one should get less than a thousand dollars. Let's make this special. Can you two work out the details? None for me, but don't forget yourselves."

***

The "thank you" checks were ready by Friday. Spencer walked through the Tenting building near the end of the first shift and distributed the checks to each employee with Jina by his side to help with the names. Spencer took in all of the employees' reactions to their bonus.

"This is wonderful. I can pay off my credit cards," said a smiling young woman.

"I can pay off my car," said another.

"My daughter will have the birthday party she asked for."

"I'm putting this in the bank," said an older man. "This will be my vacation money when I retire."

One man took a more philosophical approach. "Money is like sunshine, and we need sunshine with all of this rain we've been having."

"Enjoy your sunshine, then," said Spencer, playing along and handing him his check.

Throughout the afternoon, Spencer received many hugs and handshakes. There were even some tears shed.

A woman opened her envelope and gasped. She reached out and hugged Spencer. "You have no idea, Mr.

Ward, how much this means to me right now. My boy needs braces. He can get them now."

One young man, tall and lean with a shock of short red hair, looked at his check and stood silently off to the side, his eyes beginning to tear up.

Spencer noticed and approached. "Is there a problem?"

The young man blinked a few times to compose himself. "No, sir. I've been saving for an engagement ring so I could ask my girlfriend to marry me. Now I don't have to wait any longer. Thank you so much."

"Well, congratulations in advance." They shook hands and the young man headed toward the exit.

The same was happening at the other buildings where Roger and Steve were distributing checks. Smiles, handshakes, hugs, and tears.

Spencer made it back to his office in time to distribute the checks to the secretarial and administrative staff before they finished at five.

Gracie, his secretary, was confused. "But, Mr. Ward, I just did my job, nothing out of the ordinary."

"You're part of the team, Gracie. You deserve it as much as anyone else."

"Thank you. This is so sweet."

"Have a great weekend."

"Oh, I will!"

Steve stopped by the office after returning from the

Camping Supplies building. "I'd be willing to distribute this evening's checks if you'd like."

"That would be great. I'll do Tenting again. And Roger?"

"Oh, he'll be glad to, I'm sure. Who doesn't like handing out money? Everyone was so happy and thankful. I think I'm supposed to hug you at least fifty times, at least it was about that when I lost count of all the 'Give Mr. Ward a hug for me' directives."

"Telling me will be sufficient."

The two men laughed, and Steve left the office with a quick wave.

Spencer sat at his desk. *In the big scheme of things, the company will hardly notice the expense, but to these individuals, these families, the checks have a big impact.* Spencer looked at the photograph of his father. *Now I understand how you could be so generous. It's about making a difference.*

***

"Did you see Sunday's paper?" Steve asked when he saw Spencer in the hallway Monday morning. "Deihl's thanked an anonymous donor for allowing them to sponsor the team for the year. See, I told you I was good."

"Yes. The redundantly anonymous ninja." Spencer smiled at his own joke. "A job well done. Thank you."

They walked together to the elevator and rode together to the third floor.

"Morning, Gracie," Spencer said. He couldn't help but think he noticed a slightly more cheerful vibe from her this morning.

"Morning, Mr. Ward. And good morning to you also, Steve."

"Gracie," Steve replied, tipping an invisible hat.

The two men entered Spencer's office.

"This rain is never-ending," Steve said looking out the window. "Maybe our canoe and kayak sales will increase."

"I'd rather people buy them for fun and adventure, not out of necessity."

"True."

Spencer needed to get to work. "Can you bring up last week's sales?"

Steve opened his laptop and tapped a few keys. "Looking good. Camping Supplies keeps doing better and better. Tenting rose a little. Climbing and Boating are still selling well but haven't done as well as the others."

"That's to be expected. Our infomercial was mostly about camping. I'm tempted to do another infomercial featuring Boating and Climbing. We can certainly afford it."

"Is that something to do before summer?" asked Steve. "We only have a couple of months."

"I'll contact Jen. We'll need to find locations for the Climbing and Boating to be filmed. No such locations

on this property. Most likely, we'll hire professionals, at least for the climbing. We want it to look easy."

Spencer's cell phone buzzed. He retrieved it from his pocket. "There is a flood warning for low-lying areas along the river and for overflowing tributaries. That does not sound good."

"A warning? Usually, it's just a watch and nothing happens," said Steve. "We've never had a flood around here that I know of."

"Low-lying areas along the river?" Spencer tried to picture the scene. "A lot of farmlands will get flooded."

"And there's the park. The pavilions and bathrooms would get flooded, and many of the lower hiking trails."

They heard Roger say good morning to Gracie before he entered the office.

"Sorry I'm late, they had Bannerman Road closed to traffic. The stream was flowing over the road. The firefighters had their trucks blocking the way. One of them told me they thought the bridge was about to wash out. I had to go way around. It's not looking good out there."

"Glad you're safe," Spencer said. "We were just trying to think of what low-lying areas would get flooded. Most of the town is way above the river."

"Not on Old Route 3. There are a few old houses down there right along the river. I think a couple of trailers, too."

"Let's hope those people get out in time."

The three men turned toward the window, silently watching the sheets of rain wash over the buildings and parking lots.

***

It was difficult for Spencer to concentrate on his work. He kept being distracted by the rain pelting his window. That, and his stomach was reminding him that it was almost time for lunch.

His cell phone buzzed again. Another message. This time from the police. As of 2:00 p.m., no unnecessary travel.

"Gracie, please call all divisions and have them shut down and send everyone home. Also, have them notify the second and third shifts to stay home. Their safety is most important."

"On it, Mr. Ward. Our building, also?"

"Oh, yes, of course. Your safety is important, too. Silly me."

"I knew you meant to include us."

While Gracie was busy, Spencer used his cell phone to call his mother.

"Just checking on you, Mom. Let me know if you need anything. Don't go out. They want everyone to stay off the roads due to the flooding."

She assured him she was safe and sound, watching the local news on television.

"Love you, Mom. Bye."

He finished up the figures he was working on and tidied up the papers on his desk. He watched as the parking lots were clearing out. The colorful umbrellas moving around reminded him of dancing flowers. *Umbrella flowers dancing in the rain. I'm not usually so poetic.* The thought made him smile.

Once the lots were empty, he put on his raincoat and headed to the elevator, checking to see that everyone had gone. He stopped at the second floor and stuck his head out of the elevator. All quiet.

He checked to see that the main door locked behind him and opened his large black umbrella. Looking up, he said aloud, "You're not a very pretty flower."

***

Spencer sat at home the following day with the television on. The news was bleak. The homes along the river had washed away, just as Roger had feared. The river crested twelve feet above its normal spring flow. Several neighborhoods had minor issues with flooded basements and damaged driveways. Bannerman Road bridge did get washed out as well as a couple of others. Reporters were on the scenes filming road crews at work.

Another reporter, a young woman holding a large microphone that obscured part of her face, was interviewing an elderly woman whose trailer on Old Route 3 had washed away.

"I have nothing now," she sobbed. "My dog, two

cats, and a suitcase of clothes is all I have left." She wiped her nose with a wrinkled tissue. "I have no home, no neighbors."

The reporter explained to the viewers that all seven families that lived on Old Route 3 were safe and were being housed by the Red Cross at local hotels. Spencer breathed a sigh of relief. *Terrible, but not a tragedy,* he thought. *Thank God.*

The reporter continued, "One homeowner I spoke with was worried their insurance will not cover the complete cost of rebuilding, and his family is lucky to have flood insurance. Most of the affected families do not, making their situation even more dire. When I asked about rebuilding along the river, many said they are hesitant, and who could blame them? As one resident put it, one flood in a lifetime is enough. Unfortunately, to rebuild elsewhere means having to buy land to build on, adding to the already overwhelming expense."

Spencer caught himself thinking: *How can I help?* Plans seemed to appear in his mind so easily. *CampWild owns several large pieces of land. There's even one piece down the road from these people. I'm sure it's at a much higher elevation. As I recall, it's on the side of a hill. Maybe we could subdivide and donate the land. We could help the people rebuild. I'll have to discuss this with Steve and Roger.*

It wasn't until he had run through his plan that he realized he hadn't considered the cost. *This is so not like*

me, at least not like the old version of me, he mused. *This is so like Dad.*

CHAPTER 10
Community

"What do you think of my idea?" Spencer asked after giving an overview. "Don't be shy. I want all your thoughts."

Steve and Roger sat at the conference table opposite Spencer. Neither spoke.

Spencer continued. "Too generous?"

"On top of the million the employee bonuses just cost?" Steve asked. "I'm good with the generosity part, but as far as the company goes, it seems a bit incautious. The infomercial bubble may burst at any time, and I'd hate for us to be low on capital. But if you're okay with it, I am, too."

"That is a valid concern," agreed Spencer, "but this is one opportunity to help that I think we can't ignore. I have to have faith our income will remain high for at least the next few months."

"I have an idea," offered Roger. "What if CampWild builds the houses on company land and sells them to the families with a low monthly mortgage payment, something affordable. We'd be putting the money upfront and would get it back over time. It helps the families, but we're not losing another million."

"Donating, not losing," Spencer corrected him. "But

if we're getting the money back, it feels disingenuous to call it donating."

"You could start a trust," Roger suggested. "All of the properties would be owned by the trust, mortgages held by the trust, and payments made to the trust."

Spencer nodded. "Good idea. The trust could then use the money it gets to help others in need if there is another disaster or whatever. We could set up a board to make those decisions. Another reason to call the lawyer."

"There is no way to do all of this and remain anonymous," Roger said, shaking his head. "So how do we navigate this if we're public with it?"

Steve replied, "Technically, we are not giving anything away. The families are buying the houses. We're just making it possible."

"Let's contact the families. Maybe set up a meeting to offer our solution," said Spencer.

Steve held up a finger, pausing the momentum. "They all may not want to move into a CampWild house," said Steve.

"I have a feeling they will, at least for now." Spencer stood and crossed to his desk. "As soon as we have takers, maybe six, we'll get the necessary permits and contract with local builders. I hear there are some modular homes that are quite nice and go up quickly."

"On it," said Roger as he stood. "I'll get in touch with the families."

"And I'll speak with our lawyer," said Spencer.

"The builders are starting on Monday," Steve announced as he entered Spencer's office Friday afternoon.

"How did we get so lucky?" asked Roger. "Usually there's a long wait. It's only been three weeks."

"When the builder heard seven houses, he made us a priority."

"Did they give a move-in date?" Spencer asked.

"Because they are modulars, three months tops, the guy said. They have a big crew set to go."

"See that we continue to pay for the temporary housing while the families wait," Spencer instructed. "I don't want them worrying about that."

***

On Monday, Spencer and his two assistants arrived at the building site to watch the builders get started. They were surprised that several reporters and camera crews were also present.

"Mr. Ward. Mr. Ward," called a young woman aiming her microphone in Spencer's direction. He recognized her from the flood coverage on television.

She approached the three, the cameraman following. "Could I get a few words?"

"I've nothing prepared."

"Just a statement about what you are doing and why. This is something good happening in our community,

and our viewers need some good news, especially after last month."

Spencer cleared his throat. "Our community has been through a rough time. These families lost everything, including their homes. I've been blessed with good fortune, and I feel privileged to be in a position to help." He pointed to the field in front of him. "Seven modular homes will be built here to provide the families with high-quality housing. In this way, they can remain members of the community and not have to move elsewhere. They'll even have the same neighbors."

"Would you care to comment on the cost?" the young reporter asked.

"As I said before, I am in a position to help, and I am happy to do so." Spencer could tell from her expression that she wanted details, but he wasn't going to go there.

Other reporters clamored for his time, and he obliged each one with a similar statement. When asked by a photographer to pose with a shovel for a groundbreaking photo-op, he declined.

"This is not about me," he said.

They watched as the excavators began leveling the ground and the backhoes dug trenches to put in water and sewer lines. The foreman came over and introduced himself, but quickly returned to his work.

***

Spencer left Steve in charge of the office that

afternoon so he could attend an award ceremony at his daughter's school. Rachel was receiving an award at the spring band performance in front of the whole student body and guests. The Wards had been informed that hers was the only perfect score from their school at the recent state competition.

In the past, Spencer left these events up to his wife so often that Rachel hadn't even bothered to ask him if he would be there. *How did it come to this?* he asked himself. He knew the answer. *Work before family. Not anymore.*

He pulled into the school parking lot and saw Patty getting out of her car. They walked into the school together.

"Thank you, Spencer. This means a lot to her."

"I know."

They sat in the reserved section, away from the somewhat rowdy students. Once the performance got underway, everyone settled down. First, the chorus sang a medley of contemporary tunes. Then the orchestra performed three classical pieces.

After a short pause to reset the stage, the band wowed the audience with a rock number and two jazz tunes with many solos. Their next number, a slow-moving piece featuring Rachel and the band's other two flutists standing front and center, held the audience in silent admiration.

Spencer realized he had held his breath for the entire flute interlude.

"I didn't know she was that good," Spencer whispered to Patty. While the song finished, Spencer wondered: *What have I missed all of this time?*

After the applause faded, the band director turned to the audience.

"As you know, our students attended the state music adjudication last week. He motioned the winners to stand. "Let's give them a round of applause."

The audience clapped and cheered. The director motioned those students to sit and then continued, "It is rare that a student receives a perfect score at the adjudication. This year, we have one student who did just that, Rachel Ward." He called her forward.

The audience went wild. Several students started chanting "Rachel! Rachel!" until the director waved them to stop.

"Would Rachel's family please join us on stage?" the director asked.

Spencer and Patty stood together and walked to the steps on the side of the stage.

When Rachel saw her father, her eyes widened. "Dad?"

"Congratulations, sweetheart."

They hugged and then Rachel hugged her mother. During that time, Jay joined them from the percussion section, drumsticks in hand. Instead of a hug, he gave her a high-five, which caused boisterous laughter from the audience.

From the side of the stage, a boy carried a large trophy over to the Ward family and handed it to Rachel.

"Another round for Rachel Ward," the director said, clapping.

As the audience obliged, Rachel handed the trophy to her father and made her way back to her band seat for the final number. Spencer and Patty returned to their seats. Spencer could feel his eyes welling with tears, but he didn't care. *Family first from now on.*

***

Once Spencer and Patty returned home, they relaxed on the sofa, enjoying the quiet.

"We raised good kids," Spencer said. "Many thanks to you."

"We did our best."

Spencer wanted to tell her he knew that wasn't true on his part but kept it to himself. Instead, he said, "I worked too much."

Patty turned to him. "If we're being honest, when you took over for your father, I thought that would be the end of our marriage. Not that we would get divorced, but that you would work even longer hours and we would drift further apart, separate lives under the same roof. But something has changed about you. I can see it."

Spencer felt awkward with this talk about his personal qualities. His defense was to crack a joke.

"Maybe I'm getting better looking. Or maybe your eyesight is getting worse."

Patty tried to clarify. "Not *see it*, *see* it. I feel it. You seem more connected, kinder even. Like you were when the kids were little. You would do anything for them."

"They needed me then." Spencer quickly added, "I guess they need me now in a different way."

"They always need your love and attention, even when they don't act as if they want it."

"And what about us?" Spencer asked. "How can I fix things?"

"You already have. It's been quite a while since we've had a meaningful conversation. It feels nice. We need to keep at this."

CHAPTER 11

Ceremony

S pencer returned to his office from his weekly walk through the facility, a tradition his father started years ago to keep a connection with the employees, even if it consisted of only a smile, a nod, and a wave. Spencer enjoyed the lunches more because he got to talk to the employees and get to know them, some of them, at least.

"Congratulations, Mr. Ward," said Gracie as he entered.

"Thank you, Gracie. I guess the news of the town's award ceremony has spread."

"It has. Aren't you excited?"

"I know the town means well, so I'm happy to make them happy."

"You deserve it."

"Thank you, Gracie."

"Oh, your son called. He wants to see you. I told him you'd be back shortly. And here you are."

A few minutes later, Jay arrived.

"Hey, Jay, what brings you over here today?" Spencer asked. "It's not my birthday, is it?"

"Nope, it's work-related."

"Here to complain about your boss? Your boss's boss? Wait, wait, that's me."

"Ha, ha. No. Remember that kid who was getting picked on? The one I got suspended for?"

"Yes."

"His name is Derrick. He's looking for a summer job. I was wondering if there was a job for him here. I know I said he has Asperger's, and he says he does, but he's a good guy. We let him sit with us at lunch, and he's pretty cool once you get to know him."

"I know your Uncle Ronan is looking to hire packers in Camping Supplies. He hasn't posted yet. We'll set up an interview. Don't tell your friend he has the job. Let him go through the hiring process. It's a good experience."

"Thanks, Dad. You're the best. I better get back. Lunch break is almost over."

"You'd better. I might have to give your friend Derrick your job," Spencer said with a wink.

"Bye." Jay darted out the door.

Spencer leaned back in his chair and closed his eyes. *Did my son say I'm the best?* Spencer smiled. *My son is the best for helping someone else. His grandfather would be proud. I know I am.*

A soft knock on the office door startled him out of his reverie.

"Sorry to bother you. Headache?" asked Steve.

"No, quite the opposite. I feel great."

"You're going to feel even better when you see this." Steve held his laptop for Spencer to see. "The sales figures are in. Sales are still rising. By a lot. I don't know why I was so worried."

"It's a businessman's burden, I guess. This is great news. I'm feeling better about my new idea."

"A new product?"

"No, a new way to help the community."

"Giving more away?"

"For a good cause."

***

A week later, a large crowd had gathered at the park by the river. The flood debris was no longer scattered around, and the newly planted grass in the picnic area was beginning to show. A temporary stage, with steps on either side, sat to the right of the graveled parking area next to the new pavilion and restrooms.

Local dignitaries sat in a row at the back of the stage. Lon Smith, the town supervisor, stepped up to the microphone.

"Thank you all for coming. And thank goodness the weather is cooperating."

The crowd clapped.

"It's been a little over two months since the flood, and our crews have been busy with the restoration of our roads and bridges. I'd like to take this time to acknowledge those who went above and beyond expectations for our town." The supervisor awarded certificates of appreciation to many local residents for their part in assisting the town through the disaster.

"As you can see, our town park has new facilities. Thanks to a gift from the CampWild company and the Ward Family."

More clapping.

"Could I ask the Ward family to join me?"

Spencer, Patty, Jay, Rachel, and Ronan stood from their front-row seats and made their way to the stage steps. Spencer's mother declined to join them because of the stairs. "I'll watch from here," she said, waving them off.

"I'll sit with her," said Beth, Ronan's fiancée, as she slid over a few seats.

Spencer heard a commotion behind him as he started up the steps. He turned around to see his sister and her family following behind.

"Tina, I didn't know you'd be here."

"Surprise! Mom called a few days ago."

They took their places on the stage and the Supervisor continued.

"The Wards have also donated picnic tables and new playground equipment, which will be installed later this summer once it arrives."

More clapping.

"And now, Mr. Ward, if you would say a few words."

Spencer stepped up to the microphone. "I'm glad he said 'a few words' because I'm not a public speaker. And I'm sure you're all glad I'll be brief."

A few laughs emanated from the crowd.

Spencer pulled a paper from his pocket and unfolded it. "Thank you, everyone, for acknowledging Camp-Wild's contribution to the town's recovery efforts. I am humbled. Our police, firefighters, road crews, and medical personnel deserve praise for putting their time and energy into the town's rescue and recovery. We would be in a sorry state without them."

The audience erupted into loud applause.

"My father liked to think of his company and his community as an extended family. And what do families do? They help each other. They may not always agree, but when it matters, they help each other through the rough spots. That is what we've done, that is what many of you have done, helped each other through a rough spot.

"My family and I are wishing you a safe and happy summer. Please enjoy the park. And please, take care of each other."

Spencer stepped away from the microphone.

The Supervisor returned and raised his hand. "We are not finished. As many of you know, CampWild is building affordable houses on higher ground for the residents who lost their homes in the flood. Last Thursday, at the monthly town board meeting, the town board unanimously voted to rename the section of Old Route 3 where the new houses are being built. It will now be known as Ward Road."

As the audience cheered, Spencer looked at his family and shrugged, feeling embarrassed by the attention. He mouthed a silent 'thank you' to the crowd and motioned to the supervisor to let him back at the microphone.

"Thank you, board, for that honor. I think this would be a good time to make an announcement. Camp-Wild has been doing well lately. I see a few of our new employees in the audience. We are in the process of setting up a scholarship fund for college-bound or trade school-bound high school students. My hope is that we can provide several substantial scholarships each year to deserving students."

Spencer gave a slight bow to the cheering audience and stepped back.

The Supervisor thanked everyone for coming, and the crowd began to disperse.

***

The family returned to Spencer and Patty's house for refreshments. Tina helped Rachel bring out the chips, veggie platter, and lemonade while her husband kept their two little ones entertained.

"I don't know if I'll ever be used to speaking in public," Spencer said. "I now know why Dad liked being anonymous, even if that wasn't his main motive."

"You were fine," Tina assured him. "It was worth the trip from Portland to see my brother on the stage."

"We were all on the stage," Ronan said.

"Yes, but you, dear brother, only had a background role," teased Tina.

"Ouch," Ronan replied, laughing.

"I have another surprise," said Spencer waving a DVD. "Jen, the infomercial lady, made us a video of the outtakes and unused footage from the camping trip."

"Can we watch it?" asked Rachel. "Right now?"

"Sure."

Jay loaded the DVD into the player and the family watched, laughing and commenting through the entire show.

"Jen is making a copy for every family that attended. She said it is a thank you for being so easy to work with," Spencer said. "I think she'll have a good career ahead of her."

Beth, who was quiet most of the afternoon, spoke. "The more I get to know your family, the more I'm glad I'll get to be a part of it."

Roslyn then asked, "Do we have a date for a wedding yet?"

"Not exactly, but we are thinking October," Ronan answered. "After the summer rush and before the holiday season."

"And I know who we can ask to be the flower girl and the ring bearer," Beth added, giving Tina a look.

"I'll need time to prepare them," Tina joked. "My little monsters aren't used to performing on cue." Everyone turned to watch her children running around the

dining room table dragging pull toys behind them, laughing at the noises the toys made. "We'll work on it."

Spencer looked around at the scene in his living room. Everyone seemed happy, enjoying each other's company. He didn't feel his usual level of awkwardness. *What has changed?* he thought. *Me. I'm not stressing everyone out or being too preoccupied to be present in the moment.*

***

The afternoon wound down. Tina and her husband had taken their kids and Roslyn back to Roslyn's house. Jay and Rachel were up in their rooms. Ronan and Beth went to dinner and the movies. Patty was puttering in the kitchen.

"I'm going for a drive," Spencer called to Patty. "I'll be back in a little while."

Spencer knew where his drive would take him. To Pine Knoll Cemetery. It was only a three-mile drive, but Spencer had not made the trip since the burial. His mother had convinced him it was for the best. "Let him rest," she said. "You need to get on with your life."

This was true, but he wondered if she said that because visiting was too painful for her, and she didn't want Spencer to feel the same pain.

He parked at the entrance of the cemetery and walked up the sloped path toward his father's grave. It didn't feel right to drive through, even though it was a drivable path.

A few small clouds blocked the sun where he stood. A soft breeze kept the heat of the late afternoon air bearable. The large granite headstone in front of him was polished and new, unlike the weathered ones nearby. The grass had grown enough to cover the ground, but he dared not sit, instead choosing to lean on the stone.

Spencer closed his eyes and let the silence of the area calm his thoughts and clear his mind. A meadowlark sang in the trees at the edge of the cemetery, and another answered. The memory of his father teaching him to identify bird songs made him smile.

It was only when the clouds moved on from the sun that he opened his eyes and spoke.

"It's been quite a year, Dad. We've done so many things. You'd like how well the company is doing. Jay is still happy to be working and even got his friend a job. He's a good kid. And Rachel won a trophy for her flute playing. You always used to love hearing her play."

Spencer found it easy to talk about others. Talking about himself was a challenge. He took a deep breath.

"I've learned a lot about you since you've been gone. So many people have shared stories of your generosity. You made a big difference, more than you let anyone know. At first, I didn't understand why being anonymous was so important to you, but now I get it. It's not about you. It's about the people you help."

Spencer stood and faced the stone. "I hope you would be proud of me. I've tried to carry on your legacy.

I understand more deeply now what you meant by 'making people happy makes me happy.' I realize that I don't need to put making money over the happiness of my family. We are better now that I know that and live that. It has taken a while to get it, but having a happy family is important to me."

A small insect landed on the carved lettering, walked along for a few seconds, and flew off. Spencer watched it fly away. *Life goes on.* He turned again toward the headstone and placed a hand on the edge.

"Goodbye, Dad. I miss you."

About Doug Wing

Doug Wing has over forty years of experience in manufacturing, operations, sales, sales leadership, and executive management. He was a co-owner and vice chairman at Little Giant Ladder Systems before retiring in 2019.

Doug was a member of the senior management team that helped grow Little Giant to more than $200 million per year in sales revenue; making Little Giant Ladders the 3rd largest ladder company in the world.

In the last five years of his career with Little Giant, Doug oversaw the cable and telecom industry, and was responsible for more than $150 million in sales revenue.

He worked at Little Giant for forty-five years with his father, and other family members. In 2022 Doug published his first book, *Giant Success*. It has become a best seller on Amazon.

In 2020, he co-founded Boar Investment Group. Boar's businesses include multi-family real estate and property management.

Doug serves on the board of directors of The Honoring Heroes Foundation, a charitable organization that helps fallen police officers and their families.

He has served two missions for The Church of Jesus Christ of Latter Day Saints.

Doug enjoys riding motorcycles, playing golf, reading, and fitness. He also enjoys collecting cars and motorcycles. He was born in Schwaigern, Germany, and lives in Phoenix, Arizona.

www.dougwing.com

Don't forget to leave a review on Amazon. This story is special to me and I want to make a difference in your life by sharing one man's story of how he found new ways to find meaning in his life. He also learned the art of giving.